NDLEY • JOHN STEARNS • KEITH HERNANDEZ • ED
MILNER • CARLOS DELGADO • JEFF KENT • GREGG
TEUFEL • BUD HARRELSON • JOSE REYES • REY
RIGHT • HOWARD JOHNSON • EDGARDO ALFONZO
VIN McREYNOLDS • CLIFF FLOYD • GEORGE FOSTER
N • LEE MAZZILLI • TOMMIE AGEE • LENNY DYKSTRA
BODA • ART SHAMSKY • JOEL YOUNGBLOOD • TOM
NE • BOBBY JONES • JERRY KOOSMAN • AL LEITER
N FRANCO • TUG McGRAW • JESSE OROSCO • BILLY
VALENTINE • DAVEY JOHNSON • CASEY STENGEL
JERRY GROTE • TODD HUNDLEY • JOHN STEARNS
MAN • JOHN OLERUD • JOHN MILNER • CARLOS
MILLAN • WALLY BACKMAN • TIM TEUFEL • BUD
TER • RAFAEL SANTANA • DAVID WRIGHT • HOWARD
NE GARRETT • CLEON JONES • [barcode] NOLDS
ARLOS BELTRAN • MOOKIE WILSON • [barcode] AZZILLI
BERRY • BOBBY BONILLA • RON SWOBODA • ART
T GOODEN • RON DARLING • DAVID CONE • BOBBY
SID FERNANDEZ • BOBBY OJEDA • JOHN FRANCO

FEW AND CHOSEN

Defining Mets Greatness Across the Eras

Rusty Staub
with Phil Pepe

TRIUMPH
BOOKS

Library of Congress Cataloging-in-Publication Data

Staub, Daniel.
    Few and chosen Mets : defining Mets greatness across the eras / Daniel Staub with Phil Pepe.
        p. cm.
    Includes index.
    ISBN 978-1-60078-153-7
    1. New York Mets (Baseball team)—History. 2. New York Mets (Baseball team)—Anecdotes. I. Pepe, Phil. II. Title.
    GV875.N45S73 2009
    796.357'64097471—dc22

                                                                                        2008045498

This book is available in quantity at special discounts for your group or organization. For further information, contact:

Triumph Books
542 South Dearborn Street
Suite 750
Chicago, Illinois 60605
(312) 939-3330
Fax (312) 663-3557

Printed in U.S.A.
ISBN: 978-1-60078-153-7
Design by Nick Panos; page production by Patricia Frey
All photos courtesy of AP Images unless otherwise indicated

This book is dedicated to the 848 players who appeared in at least one game for the Mets, to the 96,732,862 fans who attended a Mets game in the team's first 46 years, and to Shea Stadium—thanks for the memories.

Contents

Foreword

As a kid, I was a baseball brat. My dad had played several years of minor-league ball in places like Wilkes-Barre; Salt Lake City; Valdosta; Oklahoma City, where he was a teammate of Al Rosen and Mike Garcia; and Houston, where his manager was Johnny Keane.

Dad was a student of the game, and he did his best to impart his knowledge to me when I was just a little kid growing up in San Francisco and learning about baseball. He would take my brother and me to Candlestick Park for the express purpose of watching the left-handed hitters that he liked.

My dad would always buy seats over the third-base dugout so we could watch the left-handed hitters. My favorite player back then was Mickey Mantle. I tried to copy him, but he was in the American League and I only saw him on television. However, I did get to see a lot of Willie McCovey. My dad loved McCovey's swing, so seeing so much of him was a great benefit. We'd sit and watch the good left-handed hitters, and Dad would instruct us, pointing out what they did as they approached the ball, their take-back and all. It was like a clinic.

One day, my dad took me to see the Giants against the Houston Colt .45s and I wondered why we were going to see them because the Colt .45s weren't a very good team. Dad said, "I want you to watch this left-handed hitter," and it was Rusty Staub.

That was the start of my association with Rusty, tenuous as it was.

Years later, I was with the Cardinals, and Rusty had come back to the National League and to the Mets after playing in Detroit and Texas. When we played each other, I tried to say hi to him, and he wouldn't acknowledge me. He was old school, a throwback, one of those guys who wouldn't talk to an opponent.

OK, fine, I thought. If that's the way he wanted it, no problem. When I came up to the big leagues, there were still a lot of those guys around who wouldn't talk to an opponent, and Rusty was one of them. And I understood that.

Then in the middle of the 1983 season, I got traded to the Mets. That was a tumultuous year for me, getting uprooted in the middle of the year from St. Louis where I had spent almost 10 years and was comfortable, going from a first-place team to a last-place team, not being where I wanted to be. It was not a very good time for me.

I was living in Connecticut, away from New York City, an hour away from Shea Stadium, and away from most of my teammates. That Mets team was so fragmented that I hardly got to know any of my teammates except Ed Lynch.

Midway through spring training in 1984, Rusty asked me where I was going to live that season. I told him I didn't know and Rusty said, "If you're unattached, you want to live in New York City. You need to get an apartment in the city. I'll show you around and acclimate you to the city. I know you're going to love it."

That's when our relationship started to develop and it became the great friendship that it is today. It was because of Rusty that I rented an apartment in New York City. Lynch was in the city, and so were Ron Darling and Danny Heap and his wife.

That season, we got into a regular routine. Before night games, the four of us would meet up at Rusty's restaurant on 73rd St. and 3rd Ave., have lunch, and then Rusty would drive us to Shea. After the game, Rusty would drive us back into the city and show us around to some of the restaurants at night.

I had come from St. Louis where everything closes early and you had to scuffle to find someplace to eat after a night game. All of a sudden, I'm in a city where I had my choice of places to eat after a night game. And, being the restaurateur and the man-about-town that he was, Rusty gave us a red-carpet introduction to the city.

By the time I got to the Mets, Rusty was mainly a pinch-hitter. The thing that impressed me about him as a player was that he was always focused on the game and focused on the pitchers.

One thing I like about Rusty is that he wouldn't do well in the diplomatic corps. I like people like that, people who will say things that are abrasive and up-front. It may tick you off, but at least you know where they stand. That's how my dad was, and I've always connected with people like that. If I've done something wrong that I'm not aware of, I'd rather have people tell me about it than have it fester. Rusty wasn't shy about telling you if he thought you were wrong. With him you always know where you stand. I like that in a person, and that's why our friendship has stood the test of time.

As a teammate, I would take advantage of Rusty's experience and, because we both hit left-handed, we would often talk hitting. You can learn things from other hitters, and I always wanted to get Rusty's take. He was a wealth of information.

I'm deeply honored that Rusty has chosen me as the number one first baseman in Mets history—especially coming from him, because I have always respected his opinion. I always made a point over the years to ask Rusty who were the greatest players whom he played against, who were the greatest pitchers, the toughest left-handers he faced, the best right-handers. Those were all the guys who were on the bubble gum cards I collected when I was a kid. After all, Rusty is 10 years older than I am, so he saw players I never did.

For me to be on that list of all-time Mets first basemen means a great deal to me. It means even more to me coming from Rusty Staub.

—Keith Hernandez

Preface

I t happened more than a quarter of a century ago, but I remember the day as clearly as if it happened last month.

The date was April 2, 1972, Easter Sunday. I was about to start my 10th major league season, my fourth with the Montreal Expos after six years with the Houston Colt .45s/Astros, and I was in West Palm Beach, Florida, the spring-training home of the Expos.

A day earlier, five days before the start of the season, as teams were getting ready to break camp in Florida and Arizona, the Major League Baseball Players Association called the first strike in professional sports history. Following the advice of the union's leadership, Marvin Miller, executive director of the MLBPA, and the player representatives, major leaguers walked out of camp.

Nobody knew what to do because it had never happened before. Some players headed home. Others waited around, hoping for a quick settlement. I was in the latter group, and that's why I was in West Palm Beach on Easter Sunday, attending mass at St. Ann's Church when who should walk in but Mets manager Gil Hodges, some of his coaches, and trainer Tom McKenna. The Mets, who trained in St. Petersburg, had broken camp, and were in West Palm Beach for their final exhibition games before flying home to start the season.

I really didn't know Hodges very well, but I always seemed to hit especially well against his Mets—just one of those quirky things that happens in baseball. In 1970, Hodges picked me for the National League All-Star team, and I had a chance to speak with him in Cincinnati, where the All-Star Game was played, and thanked him for choosing me.

Years later, I would learn from Hodges' wife, Joan, that Gil wanted me on his ballclub and had tried to get me for the Mets. It was Gil who fought for the trade that brought me to the Mets in 1972 because he wanted me to be his right fielder. Sadly, I never did get to play for him.

At one point, according to Joan Hodges, the Expos were insisting on including Tim Foli in the deal, but the Mets were balking at that and offering Teddy Martinez instead. She said Gil jumped in and said, "What's wrong with you people? Buddy Harrelson is the shortstop here. Tim Foli is never going to play. Why are you stopping me from getting the guy I want in right field because you don't want to give up a player who's never going to play here?"

Gil managed to convince his front office and when the Mets agreed to include Foli, the deal was made. I came to New York, and Foli, Ken Singleton, and Mike Jorgensen went to Montreal.

Of course, I didn't know any of this when I had a chance encounter with Hodges in St. Ann's Church in West Palm Beach on Easter Sunday, 1972.

When mass was over, I took my time leaving. I wanted to say hello to Gil because I had such respect for him, not only for what he had accomplished as a player, but also for the kind of leader he was. I caught up with him in the back of the church and we started talking, and it wasn't just a quick greeting like "Gee, it's great to see you, Gil. Happy Easter. Thanks for all the times you have been in my corner," and then you leave. We ended up talking in the back of the church for about seven or eight minutes.

What Gil and the coaches knew at the time and I didn't know was that the day before, which happened to be my birthday, the Mets and Expos had made the trade that brought me to New York, but they didn't announce it because of the strike. I had no idea when I left Gil and his coaches in that church that I was going to be a member of the New York Mets when the labor dispute was finally resolved and the 1972 season began.

I remember thinking that Easter really brings out the best in everybody as I left the church and went about my business. I did whatever it was I had to do. I had dinner with some friends that night, and after dinner, as I was driving home, listening to the car radio, I heard that Gil Hodges died that afternoon at West Palm Beach Hospital. After mass, he had played a round of golf with his coaches, and as he left the golf course, he collapsed and died of a heart attack. He was just two days from his 48th birthday. I couldn't believe it. I almost drove off the road I was so shocked by the news, thinking that I had been with him only hours before.

The official records will show that the trade that made me a Met was made on April 5, 1972, but I now know that the trade was actually made on April 1, 1972, Holy Saturday, the day before Hodges died. Because baseball was on the verge of a strike and nobody knew whether to announce the trade, or even if the trade was valid, they held the announcement in abeyance.

The trade was announced on April 5, the day of Hodges' funeral, which was less than good judgment on the part of the Mets. Instead of letting Gil be the focal point for that period, that day, that night, and the next day in the newspapers, M. Donald Grant, the Mets' chairman of the board, came out of the church and announced that Yogi Berra was going to take over as manager and that the Mets had acquired my contract from Montreal.

I was happy about being traded to the Mets and coming to New York would be the best thing that happened to me in my career. But learning how much Gil Hodges wanted me to be on his team, especially as much as I admired him, the most disappointing thing in my career was that I never got the opportunity to play for him.

—Rusty Staub

Acknowledgments

No project of this kind is possible without the help and selfless cooperation of others. For that, the authors are grateful to Keith Hernandez, who graciously agreed to contribute the foreword to this book, and to Bud Harrelson, Gary Carter, Yogi Berra, and John Franco, who were kind enough to share their insights into some of the players selected on the all-time Mets team.

The authors also wish to thank Lorraine Hamilton, director of broadcasting and special events for the Mets; Jay Horwitz, vice president of media relations; and Ethan Wilson, media relations manager for the Mets.

Thanks also to Mitch Rogatz and Tom Bast of Triumph Books for their belief in and continued support of the *Few and Chosen* series, to Ken Samelson for his unique statistical input, and to Triumph's associate editor Katy Sprinkel, for her guidance and counsel in her first venture with the *Few and Chosen* series. She is our choice for "Rookie of the Year."

Introduction

The New York Mets were conceived as the illegitimate offspring of a shotgun marriage, the product of the abandonment by two venerable New York teams and the ill-conceived and ill-fated plan to fill the void with a third league in the majors.

After the 1957 season, the Brooklyn Dodgers and New York Giants fled to sunnier climes, more expansive ballpark, and greater revenue in California—the Dodgers to Los Angeles, the Giants to San Francisco—leaving the city of New York with just one major league baseball team. The vacuum created by these defections was an enormous chasm.

For the first time in almost a century, there was no National League representative in the biggest, most vital, and most vibrant city in the United States, and it would remain so for four interminable years, a source of great deprivation for hundreds of thousands of ardent baseball fans unable and unwilling to embrace New York's one remaining major league team, the lordly and pompous New York Yankees of the American League.

In hopes of filling the void, New York City Mayor Robert Wagner established a committee whose sole purpose was to find a way, any way, to get a National League team in New York. Spearheading the search was William A. (Bill) Shea, a prominent and powerful New York attorney. The committee's options were:

- Get an existing franchise to relocate to New York (none was available).

- Enter the National League as an expansion team (there had been discussions about expansion, but the plan was tabled and there was no way of knowing when/if it would come to pass).
- Band with other cities to form a third league.

The last option seemed the most viable, and Shea concentrated his efforts there. His first move was to hook up with a renowned baseball executive, and his search led him to the resident genius of the time, the incomparable Branch Rickey, the "father of baseball's farm system" and the architect of championship teams in St. Louis, Brooklyn, and Pittsburgh.

Together, Shea and Rickey formed the Continental League, designed as a third major league to rival the established American and National Leagues, and with a New York franchise as its centerpiece. They quickly enlisted prominent sportsmen to climb aboard from Atlanta, Houston, Buffalo, Denver, and Toronto, all cities with a long and successful history in minor league baseball and now desirous of taking the big plunge into the major leagues.

Whether the hope of getting the Continental League off the ground was sincere or merely a ploy to arm-twist the major leagues into accepting its representatives as expansion teams is left to conjecture. Suffice it to say that in the summer of 1960, the National and American Leagues reached an agreement to expand from eight teams each to 10.

On October 17, 1960, both major leagues announced plans to expand. The American League would add teams in Los Angeles (to rival the Dodgers) and Washington (to replace the Senators, who were relocating to Minnesota) and begin play in 1961. The National League would also add two expansion teams but would delay their start until 1962, with teams in Houston and New York. The latter, under its official corporation name, the Metropolitan Baseball Club, Inc., (later the name would be truncated and the team would come to be called "Mets") would have as its principal owner with 80 percent of its stock, Joan Payson, a huge baseball fan and former minority shareholder of the New York Giants.

New York was back in the National League. All it needed was players, a manager and coaches, someone to run the baseball operation, and a place to play.

Coincidentally, on the day the major leagues announced plans for expansion, in New York, the Yankees held a press conference to announce that after serving as their manager for 12 years, winning 10 pennants and seven World Series, Casey Stengel was being "retired" for the unpardonable crime of reaching the age of 70.

Less than three weeks later, the Yankees called another press conference, this time to announce that George Weiss, the man who had assembled the great Yankees teams of the 1950s, was also being "retired," having reached the age of 66.

Recognizing that its fan base was likely to come from disenfranchised rooters of the Dodgers and Giants, the new team adopted as its team colors an amalgamation of the two departed New York National League teams, the Dodgers' blue and the Giants' orange.

Although the new team on the block clearly wanted to distance itself from the Yankees, it also seized on an opportunity to capitalize on the Yankees' success and, at the same time, to twit its intra-city rivals by hiring as head of baseball operations, George Weiss and as manager, Casey Stengel.

The next order of business was to find a place to play. Although plans were in the works to build a ballpark in Flushing, Queens, that structure would not be available until the 1964 season. In the interim, the Mets would play their home games for two seasons in the Polo Grounds, the ramshackle, run-down former home of the New York Giants.

The final piece of the puzzle was put in place on October 10, 1961, when the National League's expansion draft took place in Cincinnati, the National League headquarters and the site of the recently concluded World Series between the Reds and Yankees.

For the sum of $1.8 million, the Mets selected 22 players made available by the existing eight other National League teams. Their first pick was veteran catcher Hobie Landrith, selected off the roster of the San Francisco Giants. Asked why the Mets chose Landrith, Stengel explained, "You gotta have a catcher, or you're going to have a lot of passed balls."

Conducting the draft for the new team, Weiss, in the widely held belief that New York was predominantly a National League city, made it clear that he would tap into the popularity of the Giants and Dodgers and also bring in former stars of the game, names that the knowledgeable and perceptive New York fans would recognize.

Among the original 22 players drafted by the Mets were former Dodgers Gil Hodges, Don Zimmer, Lee Walls, and Roger Craig and one-time stars Gus Bell and Felix Mantilla, all with a National League pedigree. Later, Weiss would purchase or trade for former Dodgers Charlie Neal and Billy Loes, former Giants Johnny Antonelli and Jim Marshall, and Frank Thomas and Hall of Famer–to-be Richie Ashburn.

Weiss' desire to give the fans "some people they know" even extended to the broadcast booth, where he hired home-run king Ralph Kiner to join Lindsey Nelson and Bob Murphy as the Mets' first broadcast team.

The first game in Mets history was scheduled for April 10, 1962, against the Cardinals in St. Louis. Late that afternoon, a small group of Mets took the elevator on an upper floor of their hotel, the Chase Park Plaza, and began the descent to the ground floor, where they would board the team bus that would transport them to Busch Stadium. Halfway down, the elevator stalled between floors, an omen to the Mets' first season.

When the elevator was freed and finally made its descent and the players arrived at the stadium, they learned that the game had been rained out. Had they known what would transpire in the following days, weeks, and months, the Mets might have greeted news of the rainout with a victory party.

The Mets would lose nine straight games before finally breaking into the "W" column with a 9–1 victory over the Pirates in Pittsburgh on April 23. Jay Hook was the winning pitcher of the Mets' historic first victory with a complete-game five-hitter.

Victories remained scarce for the fledgling Mets, who suffered through a horrendous first year that was made tolerable only by the good humor of their lovable 72-year-old manager, the sympathetic treatment of the writers covering the team, and the ardor of their baseball-starved young fans, dubbed "the New Breed" by *New York Daily News* sportswriter Dick Young.

When the Mets won a game—rare as it was—Stengel would celebrate the sudden and unexpected success by prancing around the clubhouse proclaiming his players as "Amazin'." Soon, the phrase became a catchword for fans, reporters, and headline writers who referred to the team as "The Amazin' Mets" or simply as "The Amazin's."

When the season ended, the Mets had won only 40 games and lost 120, the most defeats ever suffered by a major league team, and finished last in the 10-team National League, a whopping 60½ games out of first place. The Mets were losers, but they were lovable losers, and their fans tolerated their ineptness because National League baseball was back in New York to stay.

In their second season, the Mets showed improvement, but it was barely perceptible. They won 51 games, lost 111 and were last again, but "only" 48½ games out of first.

The following season, the Mets moved out of the Polo Grounds into a brand-spanking-new home of their own in Flushing that would be called Shea Stadium, named for the man who led the fight to bring National League baseball back to New York.

Occupancy of Shea Stadium dovetailed with the decline of the Yankees, the bleakest period in their history. The Mets became "THE" baseball team in New York, the city's first team to draw more than 2 million paying customers. In a 12-year period, from 1964 to 1975, the Mets outdrew the Yankees every year, doubling the established Yankees' attendance for four consecutive seasons (1969-72) and certifying the belief that New York was a National League town.

They had a new home, but they were the same old Mets, as they finished in 10th place for the third consecutive year with a record of 53–109, 40 games out of first place.

Midway through the 1965 season, Stengel slipped and fell and broke his hip. From his hospital bed, the old manager anointed coach Wes Westrum to take over the reins until he could return. He never did. On August 30, Stengel announced his retirement.

"I got this limp," he explained, "and if I can't walk out there to take the pitcher out, I can't manage."

The losing continued for the Mets through their first six years, during which time they won 321 games and lost 648, finished 10th five times and ninth once. But two arrivals would change the Mets' fortunes dramatically.

In 1967, along came a 22-year-old power-throwing right-handed pitcher from California named Tom Seaver, who would win 16 games in his rookie season and would come to be known as "the Franchise."

A year later, the Mets made a deal with the Washington Senators to acquire their manager, Gil Hodges, who had been a fan idol as a player with the Brooklyn Dodgers and an original Met. Under Hodges' leadership in 1968, the Mets made a startling improvement. They still finished ninth, but they improved by 12 games over the previous year, with a record of 73-89. As if by wizardry, they had become competitive. And the best was yet to come.

In 1969, the Mets shocked the baseball world. They became the "Miracle Mets," as they improved by 27 games, won 100, and finished first in the National League East. Seaver led the way by winning 25 games and being named the National League Cy Young Award winner.

The Mets swept the Atlanta Braves in three games to win the first National League Championship Series and took on the highly favored Baltimore Orioles in the World Series. After losing the first game in Baltimore, the Mets came back to sweep the next four games and reigned as world champions in their eighth year, completing one of the most amazing turnarounds in baseball history.

Unfortunately, the Mets could not sustain the euphoria of their sudden success. Although they posted winning records in each of the next two seasons and remained competitive under Hodges, they slipped lightly and finished in third place in 1970 and 1971. But they had high hopes for the 1972 season.

However, on April 2, Easter Sunday, two days before his 48th birthday, Gil Hodges collapsed after playing a round of golf in West Palm Beach and died. Coach Yogi Berra was chosen to take over as manager for the 1972 season, which was delayed 13 days because of a strike by members of the Major League Players Association. For the third straight year the Mets finished in third place, under Berra, but the following year, with Berra cautioning that "it ain't over 'til it's over," the Mets came from last place to win their second pennant.

Berra remained on the job until midway in the 1975 season when, unable to duplicate his earlier success, he was dismissed. Roy McMillan, Joe Frazier, Joe Torre, George Bamberger, and Frank Howard ran the ship over the next seven seasons, and the Mets nose-dived once again. As they did, the Yankees enjoyed a renaissance under an aggressive new owner, George M. Steinbrenner, and a fiery manager, Billy Martin, and regained their hold on New York's fans for a period of eight years, 1976–83, until Davey Johnson arrived as Mets manager in 1984 and ushered in perhaps the most successful era in Mets history.

In seven seasons under Johnson, the Mets never finished lower than second, highlighted by their improbable comeback in 1986 when they rose from the dead to overtake the Boston Red Sox and win their second World Series. In a nine-year period, 1984–92, while the Yankees floundered once more, the

Mets became New York's favored team again, outdrawing the Yankees for those nine consecutive seasons and, in 1987, becoming the first New York team to attract more than 3 million paying customers.

With Johnson banished during the 1990 season, the Mets floundered over the next six years under Bud Harrelson, Jeff Torborg, and Dallas Green, until Bobby Valentine assumed the manager's portfolio during the 1996 season and restored order with three consecutive second-place finishes, two playoff appearances, one National League pennant and, in 2000, participation in the first all-New York World Series in 44 years (the Mets were defeated by the Yankees, four games to one).

In 2005, the Mets came full circle and entered a new era under the leadership of three New Yorkers, chairman of the board and chief executive officer Fred Wilpon from Brooklyn, general manager Omar Minaya from Queens, and manager Willie Randolph from Brooklyn.

Three years later, Wilpon, who had grown up a Dodgers fan and who had played on the same high school team as Sandy Koufax, announced plans for a new stadium to be opened in 2009. It would be called Citi Field, and it would strongly approximate the appearance of another New York City landmark, Brooklyn's Ebbets Field.

In the almost 50 years of their existence, the Mets have overcome their humble beginnings to reign as a National League powerhouse. Nine players who have played for the Mets are in the Hall of Fame—Richie Ashburn, Yogi Berra, Gary Carter, Willie Mays, Eddie Murray, Nolan Ryan, Tom Seaver, Duke Snider, and Warren Spahn—although all but Seaver and Carter were Mets only briefly and long after the prime years of their careers.

The Mets have had their share of stars in addition to Seaver and Carter; players such as Dwight (Doc) Gooden, Mike Piazza, Darryl Strawberry, Keith Hernandez, John Franco, Lee Mazzilli, and Rusty Staub made their mark as Mets.

Staub joined the Mets in 1972 after nine years in Houston and Montreal, where he became affectionately known as "Le Grand Orange." After three seasons with the Mets, Staub spent five seasons in Detroit, Montreal, and Texas before returning for a second tour of duty with the Mets in 1981. He retired after the 1985 season having set the team record for RBIs with 105 in 1975 and in pinch hits with 24 in 1983. A year after his retirement, Staub was enshrined in the Mets Hall of Fame.

A native of New Orleans, Staub made New York City his adopted home. He is among the most popular players in Mets history and among the most recognizable athletes in New York history.

After his retirement as an active player, Staub continued to be a prominent figure on the New York scene as a restaurateur and with the Mets as a front-office executive, coach, and broadcaster. In addition, he has been a driving force in several philanthropic efforts. In 1986, he founded the New York Police and Fire Widows and Children's Benefit Fund Foundation, Inc., and serves as chairman of the board of the fund which, through his efforts, has raised more than $150 million to provide tuition and financial support to the families of New York City policemen and firemen who lost their lives in the line of duty. He is the president of the Rusty Staub Foundation, which raises money to assist charities that benefit children, the elderly, and the poor. In collaboration with Catholic Charities, the Rusty Staub Foundation supports seven emergency pantries serving 650,000 meals annually to those in need.

Staub has remained associated with the Mets for the past decade as a club ambassador, representing the Mets at civic and charitable events throughout the tri-state area and can be seen frequently at Shea Stadium visiting with corporate sponsors, charitable organizations, school groups, and fans. Having entered the National League as a 19-year-old with Houston the year after the Mets came into existence, he has seen everyone who has ever played a game for the Mets and has been a teammate or opponent of most of them. As such, he is uniquely qualified to take on the challenging task of selecting the all-time Mets team.

—Phil Pepe

ONE

Catcher

It is altogether fitting and proper that I begin selection of my all-time Mets team with the catchers, because a catcher was the very first player selected by the Mets in the 1962 expansion draft and because the Mets probably have had more outstanding players at catcher than any other position.

The expansion draft to stock the two new National League franchises, the New York Mets and the Houston Colt .45s (later the Astros), was held in Cincinnati on October 10, 1961, the day after the final game of the 1961 World Series between the New York Yankees and Cincinnati Reds.

Houston had won a coin toss and was awarded the first pick in the draft. With it they chose shortstop Ed Bressoud off the roster of the San Francisco Giants. With their first pick, the Mets chose another Giant, Hobert

1. MIKE PIAZZA

2. GARY CARTER

3. JERRY GROTE

4-T. TODD HUNDLEY

4-T. JOHN STEARNS

Neal (Hobie) Landrith, a 32-year-old catcher, the veteran of 12 major league seasons. The selection of Landrith gave birth to a memorable and oft-quoted comment by Casey Stengel, who, when asked why the Mets made a catcher their first pick in the draft, replied, "You gotta have a catcher or you're going to have a lot of passed balls."

Alas, Landrith's career with the Mets was short-lived. He had played in 23 games, had 13 hits, one home run, seven runs batted in, and *three passed balls* when, on June 7, he was sent to the Baltimore Orioles as the "player to be named later" in an earlier trade that brought to the Mets Marv Throneberry, who was born to be a Met (his birth name: **M**arvin **E**ugene **T**hroneberry). Writers covering the Mets sarcastically pinned the nickname "Marvelous Marv" on Throneberry, who would come to be the symbol of the fledgling team's bumbling futility.

In later years, the Mets would thrive at the catching position. Among those who wore the so-called "tools of ignorance" in a Mets uniform were two Hall of Famers—including Yogi Berra, whose body of work with the Mets is a sampling so small (four games, two as a pinch hitter, two behind the plate, two singles in nine at-bats) as to disqualify him as a candidate for the all-time Mets team—another certain future Hall of Famer who is baseball's all-time record holder for career home runs by a catcher, a man who set the single season record for home runs by a catcher and the Mets' single-season home run record, and a defensive stalwart who artfully guided the phenomenal pitching staff of the "Miracle Mets" of 1969.

With such a formidable array of talent from which to choose, my selection of the number one catcher in Mets history is **Mike Piazza**, who gets the nod, albeit a slight one, over Gary Carter.

Piazza and Carter are similar in that each came to the Mets in well-publicized, much ballyhooed trades, some 13 years apart, when each was at the peak of his career. Their arrival immediately changed the culture around the Mets and lifted them to another level. They were the missing pieces to a puzzle that led to the Mets' run as a National League power.

Carter is deservedly in the Hall of Fame. Piazza will be when he becomes eligible. I give the edge to Piazza based on his longevity with the Mets (eight seasons compared to Carter's five) and his career offensive production (a .308 average compared to Carter's .262, 427 homers to Carter's 324, 1,335 RBIs to Carter's 1,225, and 2,127 hits to Carter's 2,092).

Mike Piazza is the poster boy for what can be achieved when hard work, determination, opportunity, and a little bit of luck. Mike was so lightly regarded as a player at Phoenixville (PA) High School and Miami-Dade North Community College that he might never have gotten his opportunity were it not for the fact that he was born in Norristown, Pennsylvania, the

Mike Piazza is one of the best-hitting catchers to ever play the game.

hometown of Los Angeles Dodgers manager Tommy Lasorda, or if Piazza's dad had not been a friend of Lasorda.

The Dodgers, at Lasorda's request and presumably as a favor to Piazza's father, drafted Mike in the 62nd round of the June 1988 amateur draft, the 1,390th pick in the country out of the 1,433 players chosen. Among those drafted in the first round that year were Andy Benes, Steve Avery, Gregg Olson, Robin Ventura, Tino Martinez, Royce Clayton, and Brian Jordan, all good players who had successful major league careers, but the only way any of them will get into the Hall of Fame is by buying a ticket.

Three days short of 10 years after he arrived with the Mets, Mike Piazza officially announced his retirement from baseball. Acclaimed as the greatest position player in the Mets' 46-year history, Piazza's announcement elicited words of praise from his former teammates, opponents, managers, team executives, and fans.

On behalf of everyone at the Mets, we salute Mike for his Hall of Fame–caliber accomplishments in our game and with our team. Mike electrified New York City and energized our franchise after we acquired him in 1998. He was an integral part of our 2000 National League Championship club. Mike played the game with passion, class, and heart—symbolic of our city.

—Fred Wilpon, Mets chairman and CEO

I got a chance to work with him for a year, and he was a joy to coach. He was a real class guy and a real team player.

—Willie Randolph, manager

You always heard about New York being a National League town. But it was easy to believe the National League was dead in New York. And then Michael showed up for work.

—Bobby Valentine, former manager

He was one of the guys who really helped me out. He was the man in New York, so to learn under him helped me out tremendously.

—David Wright, third baseman

He could definitely change the game with one swing. Nobody had his opposite-field power. Nobody!

—Billy Wagner, pitcher

He's a first-ballot Hall of Famer—certainly the best-hitting catcher of our era and arguably the best-hitting catcher of all time. I think he took some undue criticism in terms of his catching abilities. I always

> *thought he called a good game and did a good job back there. But his struggles with throwing guys out always seemed to somehow make him a bad catcher.*
>
> *—Tom Glavine, pitcher*

> *It was a privilege to watch the greatest-hitting catcher in history play the game the way it should be played and conduct himself the way a professional man should. Thank you for all of it, Mike.*
>
> *—A fan*

Five years after he was drafted, Piazza was the Dodgers' number one catcher, batting .318, hitting 35 home runs (a major league record for home runs by a rookie catcher), and driving in 112 runs. He was unanimously chosen for National League Rookie of the Year.

By 1998, Piazza was a five-time All-Star, a career .334 hitter, a three-time 100-RBI man and was generally regarded as the game's best-hitting catcher. He was a full-fledged star, and he felt he should be paid accordingly. A contract dispute arose with the Dodgers, who resolved the situation by trading Piazza to the Florida Marlins in a seven-player deal on May 14, 1998.

The Mets saw this as their opportunity to land the power hitter they desperately needed to move to the next level. Eight days after Piazza landed in Florida, he was on his way to New York in a three-for-one trade. In exchange for Piazza, the Mets sent the Marlins outfielder Preston Wilson and pitchers Ed Yarnall and Geoff Goetz.

When Piazza arrived, the Mets had gone 10 years without making the playoffs. They had finished fourth in 1996 and third in 1997. Piazza immediately changed the culture around the team almost single-handedly. After a decade of malaise, they became relevant again. People once more cared about the Mets. Fans returned to Shea Stadium largely because of him.

Piazza became the greatest position player in Mets history and, during his eight years there, he was the face of the franchise. His name appears on the team's career top 10 lists in virtually every important offensive category. He's first in slugging percentage, second in home runs and RBIs, third in total bases and extra-base hits, fourth in batting average and doubles, fifth in on-base percentage, sixth in hits, and eighth in runs.

In Mike's first season with the Mets, they missed making the playoffs by one game. The following year, they made the playoffs as the National League wild-card, and in 2000, they won the National League pennant and made it to the World Series for the first time in 14 years.

As a Mets player, Piazza batted .296, hit 220 home runs, and drove in 655 runs. Meanwhile, the three players the Mets traded away never lived up to their potential. Preston Wilson had a decent 10-year career with six teams, batting .264 with 189 homers and 668 RBIs, Ed Yarnall won just one major league game, and Geoff Goetz never rose above Class AA, so this trade is one of the best, if not *the* best, in Mets history.

In 2004, Mike hit his 352nd home run and passed Carlton Fisk for the most home runs in baseball history as a catcher.

Of the 13 catchers currently enshrined in the Hall of Fame, only Mickey Cochrane, Bill Dickey, and Buck Ewing have lifetime batting averages higher than Piazza's .308; only Fisk and Yogi Berra have more hits than Piazza's 2,127; and only Berra and Johnny Bench have more RBIs than Piazza's 1,335.

Mike gets a bad rap for his defense. I'm not saying he's in a class with Gary Carter, Jerry Grote, or some other Mets' catchers when it came to throwing runners out, bouncing on the bunt, and blocking home plate, but he certainly wasn't as bad as everybody made him out to be.

My first reaction was to make Jerry Grote number one at catcher on my all-time Mets team because he was such a tremendous defensive catcher and I have such a high regard for his work behind the plate. But when I examined the numbers more closely, because of his tremendous offense, Piazza cannot be overlooked. His numbers are incredible. They are far superior to any catcher who ever played for the Mets and are as good, or better, than any catcher in history. He was a run producer. He hit for average. He hit for power. And he was a big-game player.

One of the most memorable and most dramatic moments in Mets history was Piazza's two-run homer in the bottom of the eighth against the Braves on September 21, 2001, a blast that not only gave the Mets a 3–2 victory, but also lifted up an entire city, even a nation, in the first game at Shea Stadium after the tragedy of 9/11.

I have no doubt that when his time comes, Mike will be elected to the Hall of Fame and he will be regarded as the best offensive catcher in the history of the game. There isn't any catcher that I know of who can compare with what Mike has done. Fisk played a long, long time and he had a great career, but he doesn't have the numbers Piazza has. There are others, such as Yogi, Johnny Bench, and Bill Dickey, who played for great teams and deserve all the credit in the world. But to me, Mike Piazza is special.

As I mentioned earlier, there is a strong parallel between the arrivals of Mike Piazza in 1998 and **Gary Carter** 13 years earlier. Both came to New York in well-publicized trades in the prime of their careers and with excellent résumés, Piazza in six seasons with the Dodgers, Carter in 10 seasons with the Expos.

The Expos had signed Carter to a seven-year contract after the 1982 season but two years later decided they could no longer afford him, so they started bringing up his name in trade talks.

By 1984, the Mets were on the road to recovery after a seven-year drought in which they failed to have a winning record. I was in my second tour of duty with the Mets, and I watched as Darryl Strawberry joined the team in May 1983, Keith Hernandez arrived in a trade a month later, and Davey Johnson took over as manager in 1984. The Mets were getting better (we would win 90 games and finish second in 1984), but we still had a long way to go.

On December 10, 1984, the Mets completed a trade with the Expos, sending four young players to Montreal in exchange for Gary Carter, a seven-time All-Star, who was hailed as the final piece of the puzzle that was expected to bring a championship to the Mets. Carter, "the Kid," immediately endeared himself to Mets fans by smashing a tenth inning, game-winning, walk-off home run in his first game as a Mets player, the opening game of the 1985 season, beating the Cardinals 6–5 and sending 46,781 Mets fans home deliriously happy. We would improve by eight games over the previous season, but our 98 wins left us three games behind the Cardinals for the National League East title and out of the postseason. The best was yet to come.

The next year, Carter lived up to expectations. He hit 24 home runs and drove in 105 runs, third in the league, as the Mets won 108 games and finished 21½ games in front in the National League East. They then beat Houston in six games in the National League Championship Series and the Red Sox in seven games in the World Series—the one in which Bill Buckner booted Mookie Wilson's easy ground ball in the tenth inning of Game 6.

The Mets received a huge boost offensively from Gary Carter's bat, but it was the Kid's enthusiasm that bolstered the team in its 1986 World Series run.

It was the Mets first World Series victory in 17 years, and they did it without me. I would have liked being a player on that World Series championship team, but my playing career had ended. However, I was general manager Frank Cashen's assistant that year, so I still felt a big part of that team.

After winning it all in 1986, most people felt the Mets should have won another World Series or two, but they didn't. Part of the reason is that the years of wear and tear of catching began to take their toll on Kid. His production began to decline after 1986. He would play three more years with the Mets, then one year each with the Giants and Dodgers before returning to Montreal to end his career where it started.

When his brilliant career was concluded, Kid had played 19 seasons and caught 2,056 games, the most in National League history, which is remarkable for someone who never caught a game until he became a professional.

Unlike Piazza, when Carter graduated from high school, he was highly recruited, for both baseball and football. In football, he was a high school All-American quarterback coveted by hundreds of big-time college football programs. He had agreed to go to the University of Southern California, where he was reported to be their quarterback of the future. But when the Expos selected him in the third round of the June 1972 draft and offered him a handsome bonus, Gary declined USC's offer and opted for baseball.

Like Piazza, the Kid, who had never caught in Little League, high school, or American Legion ball, put in a lot of hard work to become one of the greatest catchers in major league history. The Kid was the whole package as a catcher: receiving, calling a game, blocking home plate. He had a great arm and was a big-time power hitter. He played only five years with the Mets and he had some good years. His greatest years were obviously with the Expos, and it was as an Expo that he went into the Hall of Fame. But you can't deny the numbers he put up with the Mets.

I go back farther with **Jerry Grote** than any other player I have known. We were kids together with the Houston Colt .45s, before they became the Astros. I was signed right out of high school as a free agent on September 11, 1961, before Houston had even played a game in the National League. I was 17 years old at the time.

Grote signed as a free agent the following June. He was 19.

So Jerry and I sort of grew up together as major league baseball players. We were in the Instructional League together. I joined the team at the start of the 1963 season when they were still the Colt .45s (they would become the Astros in 1965). Grote came up in September '63 and played in three games.

At the time, Houston had four young catchers: John Bateman, Dave Adlesh, John Hoffman, and Grote. All were terrific young prospects. They

It takes a good catcher to handle some serious stuff, and Jerry Grote handled it all—Tom Seaver, Nolan Ryan, Jerry Koosman, and plenty more. Defensively, Jerry's as good as it gets. *Photo courtesy of Getty Images.*

couldn't keep them all, so the geniuses who were running the Colt .45s picked Grote as the one to go. After the 1965 season, they sent him to the Mets for cash and a player to be named later who turned out to be pitcher Tom Parsons, a guy who never pitched another major league game. Bateman had a pretty good major league career of 10 years, six with Houston. Adlesh was a backup catcher for the Astros who came to bat only 256 times in six seasons. Hoffman got into only eight major league games.

Meanwhile, Grote played 16 seasons with Houston, the Mets, the Dodgers, and Kansas City and was, to my mind, as good as there ever was at executing all the things a catcher has to do on defense. Granted, he had great pitching staffs to work with—Tom Seaver, Jon Matlack, and Jerry Koosman and before that Gary Gentry and Nolan Ryan. Pretty good talent always makes a catcher look better, but somebody has to take credit for handling that talent.

Somebody with the Mets also has to get credit for choosing Grote over the other Houston catchers. I regret I don't know who that somebody was, but whoever it was, he certainly made the right choice.

Grote had a reputation of being ornery, but he really wasn't that way out of uniform. Jerry was two different guys, one on the field and another off the field. On the field, he played as hard as anybody, and I came to admire the work that he did behind the plate. I was happy the way he matured and became the great catcher he was.

Grote had a reputation of being ornery, but he really wasn't that way out of uniform. Jerry was two different guys, one on the field and another off the field.

The offensive side of the game always is going to be the dominant vote in making the Hall of Fame or being rated as the number one catcher in the history of any franchise. Grote didn't have the offense to go with his great defense—a .252 lifetime batting average, 39 home runs, and 404 RBIs—so he's not going to get the full recognition he deserves. That's the reason—the only reason—I have to rate him behind Piazza and Carter when it comes to picking the best catcher in Mets history.

I can't choose between **John Stearns** and **Todd Hundley** for fourth place among all-time Mets catchers, so I'll hedge a little here and pick them in a tie for fourth place.

Stearns was a little better defensively than Hundley. He was a tough guy behind the plate, a former football player who was drafted as a defensive back by the Buffalo Bills out of the University of Colorado. He was also drafted by the Phillies as the number two pick overall in the June 1973 amateur draft and, like Carter before him, decided to forgo football for baseball.

Stearns came to the Mets in a trade that sent Tug McGraw to the Phillies and John became the Mets' number one catcher, where he stayed for eight years until a broken finger and elbow tendinitis shortened what should have been a much longer career. When he was healthy, he was an outstanding catcher, a four-time All-Star and a line-drive hitter who had a career .260 average with 46 home runs and 312 RBIs. He also set a National League record for catchers in 1978 when he stole 28 bases.

Todd Hundley, a switch-hitter and the son of Randy Hundley, an outstanding catcher for the Cubs in the 1960s, had that one huge year in 1996 when he set a single-season record for catchers and a Mets single-season

John Stearns had competing draft offers from the Buffalo Bills and the Philadelphia Phillies. Luckily for the Mets, he decided to forgo a career in football for one in baseball.

record (since tied by Carlos Beltran) by hitting 41 home runs. He also drove in 112 runs. However, he never came close to those numbers again in a 14-year career, nine with the Mets, three with the Dodgers, and two with the Cubs.

I feel very good about my choices for the catching position on my all-time Mets team, but I want to make mention of others who did not make it in the top five. I have a high regard for Ron Hodges (no relation to Gil) for what he accomplished in 12 years with the Mets. Duffy Dyer was a good backup catcher for seven seasons, and Paul Lo Duca did a good job for a short time, but two seasons is not enough to consider him in the top five of all-time Mets catchers.

Todd Hundley shares the Mets' all-time record (with Carlos Beltran) for the most home runs in a single season, with 41.

Statistical Summaries

All statistics are for player's Mets career only.

HITTING

G = Games

H = Hits

HR = Home runs

RBI = Runs batted in

SB = Stolen bases

BA = Batting average

Catcher	Years	G	H	HR	RBI	SB	BA
Mike Piazza *Entering 2009, last National Leaguer to win All-Star Game MVP (1996)*	1998-2005	972	1,028	220	655	7	.296
Gary Carter *Holds National League career record for total chances by a catcher (12,998)*	1985-89	600	542	89	349	2	.249

continued	Years	G	H	HR	RBI	SB	BA
Jerry Grote *Set major league record (since tied) with 20 putouts in a nine-inning game on 4-22-70*	1966-77	1,235	994	35	357	14	.256
Todd Hundley *Only Met to catch 150 games in a season (1996)*	1990-98	829	612	124	397	11	.240
John Stearns *Selected to four All-Star Games, batted only once (1980)*	1975-84	809	695	46	312	91	.259

FIELDING

PO = Putouts

A = Assists

E = Errors

DP = Double plays

TC/G = Total chances divided by games played

FA = Fielding average

Catcher	PO	A	E	DP	TC/G	FA
Mike Piazza	5,450	330	57	41	7.1	.990
Gary Carter	3,762	284	40	48	7.2	.990
Jerry Grote	7,290	558	67	70	6.4	.992
Todd Hundley	4,082	315	43	32	6.0	.990
John Stearns	3,711	446	63	64	6.0	.985

TWO

First Baseman

So much changed around the Mets with the arrival of **Keith Hernandez** from St. Louis on June 15, 1983, primarily the culture in the clubhouse, the attitude on the field, the position in the standings, and the perception of the team as viewed by fans and opponents. For the first time in years, the Mets had a swagger.

The Mets were not a very good team in 1983. In fact, we were awful, winning only 68 games and finishing in sixth place, last in the National League East, for the second straight year. We needed a leader.

I couldn't be the leader because I was at the end of my career, a part-time player. I was no longer playing every day. A leader has to be somebody who is on the field every day. Tom Seaver was also at the end of his career and not an everyday player. Dave Kingman and George Foster were not the leader type. The rest were either too young (Darryl Strawberry, Wally Backman, Ron Darling) or at the end of their careers (Bob Bailor, Ron Hodges, Mike Torrez, Craig Swan).

1. KEITH HERNANDEZ

2. ED KRANEPOOL

3. DAVE KINGMAN

4. JOHN OLERUD

5-T. JOHN MILNER

5-T. CARLOS DELGADO

First base is more typically known as an offensive position, a place to stick a power hitter with minimal defensive risk. Keith Hernandez changed the rules at first base, making it a defensive stronghold. I have never seen anyone who has played the position better.
Photo courtesy of Getty Images.

Then Hernandez arrived. In time, Keith would become the leader on the field and in the clubhouse, but it didn't happen right away.

It's hard to fathom now when you consider what Keith became—a man-about-town, a respected veteran presence, a go-to guy in the clubhouse for the media—but when he first arrived on the Mets, he didn't like New York, and he didn't want to be here.

Keith took an apartment in Manhattan and I lived in the city, too, so I used to drive him back and forth to Shea Stadium. I kind of showed him around town a bit and told him how wonderful it was to be here. I pointed out all the incredible things you can do in New York in so many segments of life, whether it be the arts, theater, music, movies, restaurants, museums; any kind of involvement in life is here. As a result, he began to like the city. Then he *really* liked the city. And I was very happy to have been a small influence on him liking New York. I thought it was a great place for him to be, and I thought the Mets were going to benefit by him being here.

By 1984, Hernandez began to assume a leadership role with the Mets. He did it first with his play on the field. He batted .311 with 15 home runs and 94 RBIs and helped the Mets improve by 22 games and move up from sixth place to second. He finished second in the Most Valuable Player voting. Ryne Sandberg of the Cubs won it, and I thought that was an injustice. In my mind, Keith was the MVP in the league that year, maybe even more deserving than in 1979 when he shared the MVP award with Willie Stargell. Even that was debatable. Most people thought Keith should have won that one alone.

Keith first started showing his leadership the way a leader is supposed to—by doing, not saying. He did it with his defense. He was aggressive at first base. We had all those young pitchers, and Keith's aggressiveness rubbed off on them by setting an example for them and the rest of the defense. He took over the infield and played a defense at first base that very few have ever played in the history of the game.

In his first four seasons as a Met, Hernandez hit 56 home runs and drove in 357, but that's only part of what he contributed. He was a tough out in the clutch, and he got so many big hits and big RBIs for the Mets. And there was that stifling defense that brought a new dimension to the art of playing first base.

Nobody was better than Keith at defending against the bunt. He would inch up so daringly close to the batter and field bunts so quickly he made it almost impossible for a batter to successfully execute a sacrifice. I can't tell you how many times I saw him pounce on a bunt and throw to second or third base to force a runner and foil the sacrifice.

In the old days, first base was pretty much an offensive position. Often, a guy with power, but little speed and not much defensive ability, would be put on first base just to keep his bat in the lineup. There were exceptions, but for the most part the thought back then was that first base was where a guy could do the least amount of damage on defense.

That all started to change in the 1960s and 1970s. Players such as Bill White, Ron Fairly, and Wes Parker showed how valuable it was to have a good-fielding first baseman, and first base started to become an important defensive position.

In the '80s, one of the hot debates among baseball fans in New York centered on who was a better first baseman, Keith Hernandez or Don Mattingly. I didn't see a lot of Mattingly, but I saw enough of him to appreciate how good he was. I would still take Hernandez.

I have seen many great-fielding first basemen in my almost 50 years around the game, from Bill White to Ron Fairly, from Wes Parker to Don Mattingly, but nobody I have ever seen has played the position better than Keith.

Before Hernandez came, the Mets had gone through six consecutive losing seasons, but with Keith on board, the Mets' win totals jumped up. In the seven seasons he was a Met, they had six consecutive winning seasons and won their first world championship in 17 years. The year after he left, the Mets began a streak of six consecutive losing seasons.

Something tells me that can't all be coincidence.

The Mets have had better first basemen than **Ed Kranepool**, guys with more ability who have had better careers, most of them with other teams. I'm talking about people like Gil Hodges, Donn Clendenon, Willie Montanez, Eddie Murray, and Mo Vaughn, all outstanding major league players. But they were either with the Mets too briefly or they made so little impact as to be discounted when it comes to including them on my all-time Mets team.

The operative words here are "all-time Mets team." Keith Hernandez as number one Mets first baseman of all-time is a no-brainer. What he did for

Ed Kranepool (left), shown here with then-teammate Gil Hodges, was a member of the Mets' inaugural team and played there for the entirety of his 18-year career. *Photo courtesy of Getty Images.*

the Mets cannot be denied. After him, I put Kranepool. If you compare his stats against everybody else that has ever played for the Mets, it's unbelievable.

Kranepool was a Met for 18 years, longer than anybody else. He's also the only Met to play in each of the team's first 18 seasons and one of those rare players in the era of free agency and interleague trading who played his entire career with one team. He's number one on the team's all-time list in games played (1,853), at-bats (5,436), hits (1,418), doubles (225), total bases (2,047), pinch hits (90), and sacrifice flies (58) and is among the top 10 in home runs, RBIs, extra-base hits, runs, and walks.

There is a striking parallel between my career and Kranepool's. We both were signed by expansion teams as 17-year-olds right out of high school, me by Houston on September 11, 1961, and Eddie by the Mets nine months later on June 27, 1962. We were both young, left-handed hitting first basemen.

Both of us would have no doubt benefited by playing a few years in the minor leagues where we could learn our trade and gain valuable experience, but the Mets and the Colt .45s were eager to find a young, homegrown player around whom to build a team. Kranepool was particularly desirable by the Mets because he grew up in New York and starred at James Monroe High School in the Bronx, which had produced the great Hall of Fame slugging first baseman of the Detroit Tigers, Hank Greenberg.

Kranepool is the youngest player ever to play for the Mets. He was just 17 years, 10 months, and 14 days old when the Mets brought him up.

Kranepool is the youngest player ever to play for the Mets. He was just 17 years, 10 months, and 14 days old when the Mets brought him up after only 41 games in the minor leagues, and he got into three games for them in their first season, 1962. He batted six times and had one hit, a double. I'm not sure getting to the big leagues was good for Kranepool's development, but he played. I didn't get to Houston until April 1963. I'm not sure that was good for me, but I survived.

Early in our careers, Eddie and I often were compared to one another. We were the yardstick by which the progress of the two National League expansion teams were measured, so it was ironic that we would become teammates when I was traded to the Mets in 1972. We would play together for four seasons.

As cantankerous as Eddie could sometimes be, I really liked him a lot. I still do. He did a good job for the Mets organization. He was someone they could promote when the team was bad, and when the Mets got good, he made an important contribution. In the "Miracle" year of 1969, platooning with Clendenon at first base, Eddie hit 11 home runs, drove in 49 runs, and hit a home run in Game 3 of the World Series.

Toward the end of his career, Eddie was a valuable and skillful pinch-hitter, which, I can say from experience, is no easy job.

Kranepool got his just reward when he was elected to the Mets Hall of Fame in 1990.

Dave Kingman, as we all know, could be his own worst enemy. He could run, he could throw (he was a pitcher in college), and he could hit with as much power as anybody ever hit. But his disagreeable personality and his surliness toward the media prevented him from becoming as big a star as his ability would have permitted.

Dave Kingman was a long-ball hitter. Period.

Kingman never was a hitter for average, and he never was very good at the little things. Kingman hit the bomb, period. That's what David did, and you can't take it away from him.

I was there in Fort Lauderdale in the spring of 1975 when Kingman hit the longest home run in the history of the world against Catfish Hunter. It was the damnedest thing I ever saw. The wind was blowing about 35 miles an hour straight out to left field, and that ball wasn't even thinking about slowing down when it left the ballpark. They found the ball the next day, across left field and resting on the infield of the practice field beyond the main field. Estimates on the distance the ball traveled ranged as high as 600 feet.

He was not a good defensive player, but he could hit. When you look at the numbers he put up with the Mets, he deserves this place on their all-time team. I'm talking about 154 home runs in 664 games as a Met, covering 2,323 at-bats. That averages out to one home run in every 4.3 games and one home run in every 15 at-bats, numbers that are almost Ruthian. (The Babe, for his career, had one home run in every 3.5 games and one home run in every 11.7 at-bats.)

You can talk about any hitter in history, Babe Ruth, Mickey Mantle, Reggie Jackson, Willie McCovey, Mark McGwire, Barry Bonds.... Kingman hit the ball as hard and as far as anybody.

Although he played only three seasons for the Mets, **John Olerud** certainly made an impact in that time with 63 home runs, 291 runs batted in, and an average of .315 that makes him the Mets' all-time career batting leader.

Olerud was an outstanding but underrated player for 17 seasons with five teams. He finished his career with excellent numbers—a .295 career average, 255 home runs, more than 2,200 hits, and more than 1,200 RBIs. All he did was hit, field, and be a good teammate.

The one thing Olerud didn't do well was run, but everything else he did exceptionally well. He went about his job very professionally, and for that I admired him a great deal. He wasn't a big home-run hitter, but he was a run producer. He's another guy, like Hernandez, who could get that tough RBI. I respected him a lot, and he was a great influence on the team in his short time with the Mets.

It seemed as if one minute John was here, and the next minute he was gone, which kind of sums up his personality. He didn't have an ego. He didn't make waves. He didn't make headlines. He didn't get involved in controversy. He never said anything dumb. He just did his job quietly and efficiently.

John Olerud had a lot of great years with other teams, but he holds the Mets' record for career batting average, hitting .315 over his three seasons in New York.

*I*f ever a player was born to be a Met, it was **M**arvin **E**ugene **T**hroneberry, upon whom writers covering the team sarcastically pinned the nickname "Marvelous Marv" and who came to be the symbol of the early franchise's struggles.

Throneberry was a promising young left-handed power hitter who was signed by the Yankees in their belief that he would be a threat to reach Yankee Stadium's short right-field fence. He came up through the Yankees' farm system and reached the Bronx in the late 1950s.

If imitation is the purest form of flattery, it was obvious to all that Throneberry idolized Mickey Mantle. His left-handed swing was patterned after Mantle's. He walked like Mantle, wore his uniform like Mantle, ran like Mantle, and even affected Mantle's speech pattern. Unfortunately, he couldn't hit like Mantle.

In 141 games with the Yankees, Throneberry hit only 15 home runs. He was part of a package sent to Kansas City in a deal that brought Roger Maris to the Yankees.

By 1962, Throneberry was a member of the Baltimore Orioles when the Mets realized they could not depend on an aging Gil Hodges, plagued with a bad knee, to play the entire season at first base. On May 9, Throneberry became a Met.

Almost immediately, Throneberry endeared himself to Mets fans with his power (he was second on the team with 16 home runs and fourth with 49 RBI), and they were willing to overlook his strikeouts (83 in 357 at bats) and his misadventures in the field and on the bases.

On June 17, Throneberry hit a triple against the Cubs but was ruled out for failure to touch first base. When Casey Stengel limped out to argue the call with the second-base umpire, he was cautioned by first-base coach Cookie Lavagetto to go easy.

"Don't argue too much, Case," said Lavagetto. "I think he missed second base, too."

After **John Milner** hit 17 home runs as a rookie, the Mets switched him from the outfield to first base and believed they had a young star in the making who would hold down the position for a decade or more and become a big home-run hitter.

John stayed with the Mets for seven seasons, and although he did hit 94 home runs and was a productive player for them and the regular first baseman on the 1973 National League championship team, he never became the huge star they thought he would be. Milner had some raw talent, but he was hampered by hamstring injuries.

The Mets drafted Milner in the 14th round of the June 1968 amateur draft. He was from Atlanta, and he grew up idolizing Henry Aaron. Although he was left-handed, John copied Aaron's batting style and even acquired Aaron's nickname, "Hammer."

I have one unforgettable memory of Milner. It was early in John's career, and we were in spring training, sharing the ballpark in St. Petersburg with the Cardinals and playing the Cards in an exhibition game. Bob Gibson was

John Milner was a solid-hitting first baseman, but injuries hampered him from having the sort of career numbers he might have had. *Photo courtesy of Getty Images.*

the starting pitcher for St. Louis, and the plan was for him to pitch five innings.

The first time up, Milner hit a rocket for a double. The second time up, he hit another rocket for a triple. Then it was the fifth inning, Milner was scheduled to lead off, and I was hitting right behind him. Before the inning started, I went to manager Yogi Berra and his coaches, and I said, "I don't know this young man (Milner), but I do know Gibby and he's going to drill him. You better tell him to be loose because Gibson's going to hit him. I know it."

"Nah," Yogi said. "It's spring training. He's not going to do that."

I said, "I rest my case. You guys are crazy. Gibson's going to take him out, so help me."

First pitch, Gibson hit Milner in the ribs. Poor Milner was standing up there trying to get his hacks in, and he had no idea he was going to get it.

My only comment was, "Oh, it's only spring training."

I was up next, and I thought Gibby was going to hit me, too. I thought he might be so teed off that he'd get both of us. He didn't, but I was ready just in case.

After the 1977 season, the Mets decided it was time to cut bait with Milner and stop waiting for him to become a big-time power hitter for them. They included him in a four-team trade with the Pittsburgh Pirates, Texas Rangers, and Atlanta Braves.

Milner wound up in Pittsburgh, and the Mets got Willie Montanez, another of the many stopgaps the Mets would employ at first base, a position that would be a problem area for them for much of the 1970s and the early 1980s until Keith Hernandez arrived.

The final chapter of **Carlos Delgado**'s career has yet to be written, but what he has produced so far (469 home runs and 1,489 RBIs) makes him a borderline Hall of Fame candidate.

What he produced in his first three years as a Met (100 homers and 316 RBIs) gives him a place on my all-time Mets team, tied for fifth at first base with what they call in the music world, a bullet (that is, moving up).

Before he came to the Mets in a trade with the Florida Marlins in 2006, Delgado had seven seasons of more than 100 RBIs with the Marlins and Toronto Blue Jays, three seasons with more than 40 homers, and nine with 30 homers or more.

Carlos Delgado, who was traded to the Mets in 2006, provides some serious power in the Mets' recent lineups. *Photo courtesy of Getty Images.*

He also had two monster years—2000, when he hit 41 homers, drove in 137 runs, batted .344, and was voted Major League Player of the Year, and 2003, when he batted .302, hit 42 homers, drove in a league-leading 145 runs, and was second in the American League Most Valuable Player voting.

In 2007 with the Mets, a hand injury caused Carlos to fall off to 24 homers and 87 RBIs and when, at age 36, he got off to a slow start in 2008, people were predicting that his career was coming to an end. But Delgado came on strong in the second half to finish with 38 homers and 115 RBIs and was as responsible as any Met for the team's second-half surge that left them one win away from making the playoffs.

Statistical Summaries

All statistics are for player's Mets career only.

HITTING

G = Games

H = Hits

HR = Home runs

RBI = Runs batted in

SB = Stolen bases

BA = Batting average

First Baseman	Years	G	H	HR	RBI	SB	BA
Keith Hernandez *Had .357 career average with bases loaded*	1983-89	880	939	80	468	17	.297
Ed Kranepool *Hit pinch-hit double in final at-bat of career, 9-30-79*	1962-79	1,853	1,418	118	614	15	.261
Dave Kingman *Slammed 8 career homers against Steve Carlton, his most against any opposing pitcher*	1975-77, 81-83	664	509	154	389	29	.219

continued	Years	G	H	HR	RBI	SB	BA
John Olerud *Hit .438 in 1999 Division Series vs Diamondbacks*	1997-99	476	524	63	291	5	.315
John Milner *Hit 3 grand slams for Mets in 1976*	1971-77	741	586	94	338	20	.245
Carlos Delgado *Belted 38 homers for the Mets in both 2006 and 2008*	2006-08	442	440	100	316	5	.265

FIELDING

PO = Putouts

A = Assists

E = Errors

DP = Double plays

TC/G = Total chances divided by games played

FA = Fielding average

First Baseman	PO	A	E	DP	TC/G	FA
Keith Hernandez	6,997	783	40	635	9.2	.995
Ed Kranepool	10,492	779	72	900	8.7	.994
Dave Kingman	2,726	182	40	227	8.2	.986
John Olerud	3,894	341	21	371	9.2	.993
John Milner	2,911	205	22	267	8.6	.993
Carlos Delgado	3,569	249	24	301	8.9	.994

THREE

Second Baseman

My choice of **Jeff Kent** as the number one second baseman in Mets history over such other established second basemen as Felix Millan, Doug Flynn, Wally Backman, Tim Teufel, Ken Boswell, Gregg Jefferies, and Ron Hunt may be surprising to some.

The perception that Kent was here only a short time and produced little as a Met is a misconception. Kent was a Met for three full seasons and part of two others, a total of 498 games, more than Hunt, Teufel, and Jefferies. If you look at his stats with the Mets, he dwarfs everybody else who ever played second base for them. Kent hit more home runs (67) and drove in more runs (267) than any other Mets second baseman and had a higher batting average than any other Mets second baseman.

1. JEFF KENT

2. GREGG JEFFERIES

3. FELIX MILLAN

4. WALLY BACKMAN

5. TIM TEUFEL

Kent was drafted by the Toronto Blue Jays in the June 1989 amateur draft and was traded three years later to the Mets in exchange for David Cone. Although he put up good offensive numbers, the Mets kept trying to find someone whom they liked better at second base and kept trying to convert Kent into a third baseman. That didn't go over very well with Jeff, a man of

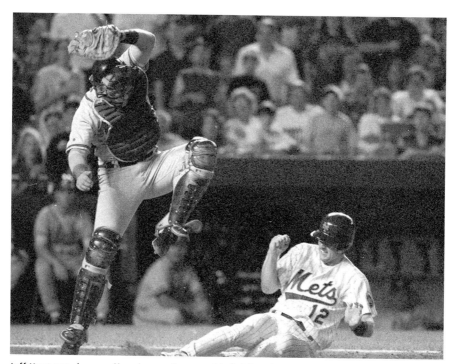

Jeff Kent may have suffered some lapses with fielding, but his offensive production more than made up for them.

enormous pride and iron will. He fought to stay at second base. He knew he was an All-Star second baseman, but as a third baseman he might have been just another guy. This difference of opinion led to strained relations between Kent and the Mets.

Eventually they came to a parting of the ways, and Jeff was sent to Cleveland in a deal that brought Carlos Baerga, a bona fide second baseman, to New York. Practically from the minute he put on a Mets uniform, Baerga's career went into a tailspin. After 2½ seasons with the Mets, Baerga became a free agent, and the Mets never even made him an offer.

Meanwhile, more than a decade after the Mets traded him, Kent, now with his sixth team, was still putting up big numbers and still playing second base.

I am baffled by why the Mets were so hell-bent on moving him to third base. Kent was never going to be a Gold Glove second baseman, but I thought he did a decent job defensively, and he figured to get better, which he did. He's a tough, hard-nosed guy, the son of a former California motor-cycle cop, and he has always played the game the right way and without fear. He hangs in as well as anybody turning the double play. His desire and his bat can't be denied. My feeling is that when you have a player at what is primarily a defensive position like second base and he puts up the offensive numbers Kent has produced, you don't mess with him. You leave him there if that makes him happy, and you live with his defensive lapses because his bat will more than make up for them.

Not letting Kent stay at second base, where he wanted to be, may be one of the biggest mistakes the Mets ever made. They could have had an All-Star second baseman for years, a guy who could hit 25 to 30 home runs and drive in 100 runs a season, someone who has driven in more runs and hit more home runs than every one of the 17 second basemen in the Hall of Fame (he passed Ryne Sandberg for the record for home runs by a second baseman when he belted his 278th in 2004). Kent has more hits than Hall of Famers Bobby Doerr, Johnny Evers, Billy Herman, Tony Lazzeri, Bill Mazeroski, Bid McPhee, Jackie Robinson, Red Schoendienst, and Sandberg and a higher lifetime batting average than Doerr, Evers, Nellie Fox, Mazeroski, McPhee, Joe Morgan, Schoendienst, and Sandberg.

Through the years, Kent has acquired the reputation of being something of a malcontent, a loner, a tough guy to handle, unfriendly, irascible, and unapproachable. Maybe that's all true; maybe it's not. I really don't know. What I do know is that I'll gladly take a team full of guys who hit like he does and play the game like he does.

When I was no longer a player and was working for the Mets organization in a variety of roles—assistant to the general manager, member of the broadcast team—Mets general manager Frank Cashen would occasionally ask me to take a particular personal interest in a young player who might be having some problems, either on the field or off. I would start talking to the player in spring training, just off-the-cuff stuff, a former player talking to a young player, all of it on the QT. It wasn't something that anybody knew about.

One year it was Kevin Mitchell, another year it was Wally Backman, and one year it was **Gregg Jefferies**. Early in his career, after getting off to a quick start, Jefferies went into a horrendous batting slump and Cashen said to me, "Why don't you talk to him and see if you can help him?"

Gregg Jefferies was a two-time All-Star, but he never did reach the potential that the Mets had hoped for when they signed him on to be the new face of the franchise. *Photo courtesy of Getty Images.*

I told Cashen that if I did, Bill Robinson, the Mets' hitting coach, would hate me for the rest of my life if the kid would give me any credit. I said, "It's not my job to help younger players, and I don't want someone whose job it is to take offense and accuse me of meddling."

But Cashen insisted. "Let's just see if we can do this quietly," he said.

So one day Cashen brought the kid in, and we sat down and started talking. I told Jefferies, "Here's the rule. I don't care if you start hitting .600, you're doing it on your own. I have nothing to do with it. My name cannot be mentioned. Is that understood?"

"Yes," Jefferies said.

He didn't hit .600, but he hit about .450 for about six weeks, and at one point, the media surrounded him and he let it out that I had been working with him. Naturally, that became a story for the writers, and from that day forward, Bill Robinson and I were no longer friends. So that ended it. I couldn't do it anymore.

Jefferies was a kid who wasn't very well liked by his teammates. They thought he had too high an opinion of himself. He wasn't a bad kid, but he was young and immature, and if he had a high opinion of himself, it was understandable. What athlete in his position *wouldn't* have a high opinion of himself? He had been Minor League Player of the Year two years running, and the Mets didn't help the situation. When Jefferies was a rookie, they put him on the cover of the team's annual yearbook because they were trying to promote him as the future of the Mets. Although Gregg had nothing to do with the choice, it hurt him and caused him a lot of problems with certain veterans on the team who apparently felt slighted.

As a result, Gregg came to be looked upon negatively by his teammates. It wasn't entirely his fault, although he did say some stupid things from time to time, again much of it out of immaturity. I always thought some people could have helped him get past that reputation, but the people who could have helped him were the same people who resented him and were getting on his case.

The bottom line is that Jefferies had a great deal of ability, and he could have been really good. He did do well—it's not as if he had a bad career. In five seasons with the Mets, he batted .276, hit 42 home runs, and—although he wasn't a home-run hitter but more of a line drive–type hitter—drove in 205 runs. Among Mets second basemen, only Kent had better numbers.

Gregg went from the Mets to play with the Royals, Cardinals, Phillies, Angels, and Tigers, 14 seasons in all. He moved around from second base to third, first, and the outfield and had a career batting average of .289 with 126 homers and 663 RBIs. He made the All-Star team twice. In 1993, playing first base for the Cardinals, he batted .342 and finished third in the National League in batting.

That's a pretty good career, but in all honesty, it could have been, and probably should have been, a whole lot better.

I loved **Felix Millan** as a player. If you were to take his entire career, you'd have to put him right up there with Jeff Kent among Mets second basemen, but our focus here is strictly about their performance as a Met, and Millan's offense doesn't measure up to Kent's, or even Jefferies', for that matter.

Felix's defense was another story. With the glove, he might have been the best the Mets ever had, but as I previously stated, voters for the Hall of Fame and Most Valuable Player usually look only at the offensive side of the ball, so I guess, except in rare cases, that should continue as the barometer in picking an all-time team.

Millan had played seven seasons with the Braves when they traded him to the Mets with lefthander George Stone for right-handers Danny Frisella and Gary Gentry in one of the best trades the Mets ever made. It came after Felix had batted .257 in 1972, a drop of 32 points from the previous season. Although he was only 29 at the time, the Braves probably figured he was on the downslide.

It's not a coincidence that after Millan left Atlanta, the Braves went into a funk that would last a decade and that when he arrived in New York, the Mets went on the upswing. Millan teamed with shortstop Buddy Harrelson to form one of the best double play combinations in the game.

Felix the Cat did not possess the offensive potency of Kent or Jefferies, but he was an outstanding hitter, one of the toughest players in the National League to strike out. He choked way up on the bat, a style of hitting you never see any more. In 1973, his first season with the Mets, Millan rebounded to hit .290, struck out only 22 times in 638 at-bats, and solidified the Mets' infield defense. He fielded .989, made only nine errors, and helped the Mets

Spirit of '76—the Mets' formidable infield: (from left) Roy Staiger, Bud Harrelson, and Felix Millan. *Photo courtesy of Getty Images.*

stage a second-half surge that saw them come from last place to win their second National League pennant.

Millan played five seasons with the Mets, but once his production began to decline in the 1977 season, Felix chose to retire rather than hang on. He was only 33 at the time. He left the game a three-time All-Star and a two-time Gold Glove winner with a lifetime batting average of .279 and a lifetime fielding average of .980. In 5,791 at-bats, he struck out only 242 times, or one strikeout for every 23.9 at-bats, which makes him the 56th toughest player to strike out in the history of baseball of those players with a minimum of 3,000 plate appearances.

Second baseman Ron Hunt was the Mets' first bona fide All-Star. Hall of Famer Rich Ashburn actually was the Mets' first All-Star in 1962, but that was not so much an honor earned as it was ceremonial. Although he would bat .306 for the Mets in the final year of a brilliant 15-year career, 12 of them with the Philadelphia Phillies and two with the Chicago Cubs, Ashburn was chosen on the 1962 National League squad because baseball had mandated that every major league team had to be represented in the All-Star Game.

Hunt also became the first Mets player to start an All-Star Game when he was elected by fans at second base over future Hall of Famer Bill Mazeroski for the 1964 game, which was played in brand-new Shea Stadium on July 7. Hunt proudly took his place alongside his more prominent National League teammates Roberto Clemente, Willie Mays, Billy Williams, Orlando Cepeda, Ken Boyer, and Joe Torre.

In his first at-bat, leading off the bottom of the third inning, Hunt thrilled the partisan Shea crowd of 50,850 by lining a solid single against the American League's starting pitcher, Dean Chance. He would play the entire game at second base, later grounding out against Camilo Pascual and striking out looking against reliever Dick "the Monster" Radatz. In his only defensive play, Hunt grabbed a bunt on the fly off the bat of the legendary Mickey Mantle.

Hunt had become a Met after the 1962 season when his contract was purchased from the Milwaukee Braves. With an old-fashioned, aggressive style of play symbolized by belly-flop slides and a perpetually dirty uniform, Hunt quickly became a fan favorite and a reason for future hope on a dismal team laden with over-the-hill, aging players and rejects from other teams.

In 1963, his rookie season, 22-year-old Hunt batted .272 with 10 home runs and 42 RBIs; led the Mets in batting, runs, hits, and doubles; was named their Most Valuable Player; and finished second in the voting for National League Rookie of the Year to another second baseman by the name of Pete Rose.

Hunt spent four productive seasons with the Mets and was traded after the 1966 season to the Dodgers with outfielder Jim Hickman for

Tommy Davis, a former National League batting champion and a Brooklyn native.

Hunt moved from the Dodgers to the Giants, Expos, and Cardinals, where he continued to put up good numbers, continued to get his uniform dirty, and perfected getting hit by a pitch to an art form, leading the National League in that dubious and painful distinction for seven consecutive seasons, 1968–74.

As a Mets rookie, Hunt was plunked 13 times, second in the National League to Frank Robinson. With the Giants in 1968, he was hit 25 times. Three years later with the Expos, he established a still-standing modern major league record by getting hit 50 times in a season and three times in one game. On the plus side, he also set an Expos record by hitting into only one double play in 520 at bats. Two years after that, he set another Expos record by striking out only 19 times in 401 at bats.

When he retired after the 1974 season, Hunt held the major league record for getting hit by a pitch with 243 (later broken by Don Baylor and Craig Biggio), had a career batting average of .273, and had struck out only 382 times in 5,235 at-bats (one strikeout for every 13.7 at bats).

It would be natural for Mets fans to think of **Wally Backman** and **Tim Teufel** as one entry, 4A and 4B among second basemen, because they were tied together so closely. They were a platoon at second base, and together they were a special thing for the World Series champion 1986 Mets. But Backman deserves to be rated a notch higher than Teufel because he got there first, stayed there longer, and put up better numbers.

The Mets made Backman their number one pick, the 16th overall, in the June 1977 first-year draft. Three years later, Wally reached New York, and although he hit well, his mediocre defense kept him from being the regular second baseman and he kept getting sent down to the minor leagues.

At Tidewater in 1983, Backman's manager was Davey Johnson, who was impressed with Wally's aggressive style of play, as well as his bat. When Davey was made manager of the Mets in 1984, he brought Wally with him and made him his starting second baseman.

At first, Backman batted leadoff, but when Lenny Dykstra arrived, Johnson put Lenny in the leadoff spot and dropped Wally to the number two batting position, which was his perfect spot. He was a switch-hitter with speed and a high on-base percentage. He could bunt, hit and run and take pitches to allow Dykstra to steal. It was as if Lenny and Wally were soul mates, two parts of a whole, similar in their aggressive style of play. They complemented one another perfectly and even came to be known as the Mets' "Partners in Grime," because they played hard, played to win, and were never afraid to get their uniform dirty.

I cared a great deal about Wally. He was a little gamer. He just busted it every game. I guess he grew up a little tougher than other people. Backman was what we call a "grinder," a guy who would do anything to win, and he seemed to save his best for big games.

Backman was what we call a "grinder," a guy who would do anything to win, and he seemed to save his best for big games.

Wally Backman was a natural number two hitter, a switch-hitter with a monster on-base percentage who could bunt, hit and run, and do whatever it took to move the runners. *Photo courtesy of Getty Images.*

Tim Teufel (center) and teammates put on their rally caps during Game 6 of the 1986 World Series. Teufel and Wally Backman platooned at second base throughout the championship season.

In the championship season of 1986, Wally batted .320. In that incredible National League Championship Series against the Astros, he led in runs scored with five.

In Game 3 of the NLCS, with the Mets trailing 5–4, he led off the bottom of the ninth with a bunt single and scored on Dykstra's game-winning, walk-off home run.

In Game 5, with the score tied 1–1 and one out in the bottom of the twelfth, he reached base on an infield hit, went to second when he caused Charlie Kerfield to throw wildly attempting to pick him off at first, and scored the winning run on Gary Carter's single.

And in the unbelievable Game 6, which many have called the greatest baseball game ever played, Wally's single in the top of the fourteenth inning put the Mets ahead, 4–3. The Astros tied it in the bottom of the fourteenth and in the top of the sixteenth, the Mets rallied for three runs, Backman scoring the third run, which became the winning run when the Astros scored two in the bottom of the inning.

In the World Series victory over the Red Sox, Backman scored four runs and batted .333.

When Gregg Jefferies came along and the Mets decided he was going to be their second baseman of the future, they traded Backman to Minnesota.

For all he contributed to the success of the Mets in the mid-1980s—his aggressiveness, his speed, his ability to get on base—the one weakness in Wally Backman's game was that he was not a very good right-handed hitter. As a result, the Mets figured they needed a right-handed hitting second baseman to platoon with Backman.

Prior to the start of spring training, 1986, the Mets acquired Tim Teufel from the Minnesota Twins in a five-player trade. In the deal, the Mets sent Billy Beane to Minnesota, the same Billy Beane who is the *Moneyball* guru and has become the brains behind the success of the Oakland Athletics.

Being the high-energy, fierce competitor that he was, Backman hated the idea of platooning, but it worked out for the Mets. Splitting time at second base, Backman and Teufel combined for five home runs, 58 RBIs, and 102 runs, and the Mets won their second World Series.

Teufel remained with the Mets for six seasons, hit 35 homers, and drove in 164 runs. Tim did a lot of things for the Mets and in fewer at-bats than some other second basemen. There were others with better numbers than Teufel, but being part of a World Series championship team, even as a platoon player, elevates his stature in my mind.

Toward the end of his career, Teufel became a right-handed bat off the bench. When he retired, he returned to the Mets as a minor league instructor, coach, and manager.

Statistical Summaries

All statistics are for player's Mets career only.

HITTING

G = Games

H = Hits

HR = Home runs

RBI = Runs batted in

SB = Stolen bases

BA = Batting average

Second Baseman	Years	G	H	HR	RBI	SB	BA
Jeff Kent *Doubled for the Giants' only hit vs. Bobby Jones in final game of the 2000 Division Series*	1992-96	498	510	67	267	12	.279
Gregg Jefferies *Had series-high 9 hits in 1988 NLCS vs. Dodgers*	1987-91	465	472	42	205	63	.276
Felix Millan *First Met to play 162 games in a season (1975)*	1973-77	681	743	8	182	11	.278

continued	Years	G	H	HR	RBI	SB	BA
Wally Backman *Had league-leading 14 sacrifices in 1985*	1980-88	765	670	7	165	106	.283
Tim Teufel *Had two doubles and two home runs in a game at Cincinnati, 7-5-87*	1986-91	463	328	35	164	6	.256

FIELDING

PO = Putouts

A = Assists

E = Errors

DP = Double plays

TC/G = Total chances divided by games played

FA = Fielding average

Second Baseman	PO	A	E	DP	TC/G	FA
Jeff Kent	777	1,085	45	231	4.9	.976
Gregg Jefferies	602	725	31	109	4.1	.977
Felix Millan	1,671	1,648	71	386	5.0	.979
Wally Backman	1,177	1,661	60	325	4.3	.979
Tim Teufel	510	722	34	138	3.9	.973

FOUR

Shortstop

Bud Harrelson was never going to dazzle anyone with his physical presence—he was listed officially as 5'11" and 160 pounds, which may be slight exaggerations. He didn't dazzle the team he rooted for as a youngster growing up in north California, either. When the San Francisco Giants rejected him as "too small," Buddy signed with the New York Mets. Neither are Harrelson's career statistics going to impress anyone: a .236 batting average, seven home runs (in 4,744 at-bats) and 267 runs batted in.

But statistics don't always reveal the real worth of a player. To truly appreciate Bud Harrelson, you had to see him every day, day in and day out, as I did for four straight years from 1972–75. I'd put Harrelson out there at shortstop anytime. Ask Tom Seaver who he'd want playing shortstop behind him. I'm guessing he'd pick Harrelson, and Tom had two other outstanding shortstops behind him, Dave Concepción with the Reds and Ozzie Guillen with the White Sox.

Buddy was as professional a player as I've ever been around. I don't know of any player I've ever been around who approached his job any better than

1. BUD HARRELSON

2. JOSE REYES

3. REY ORDONEZ

4. KEVIN ELSTER

5. RAFAEL SANTANA

Bud Harrelson was the definition of hardworking. He played 13 seasons with the Mets and ranks on their all-time lists in games played, at-bats, triples, hits, stolen bases, and runs scored. *Photo courtesy of Getty Images.*

48

he did. He didn't say much; he just went out and played. And he was a winner. That's the true measure of a player.

Buddy was relentless in his discipline. He went about working correctly, and he worked a lot. Harrelson had great speed, great range, and a great arm, and he seemed to be instinctive about being in the right place at the right time. He studied opposing hitters and his own pitchers. He knew how his pitchers were going to attack hitters and positioned himself accordingly, which he did as well as anybody.

Buddy wasn't a great hitter, a switch-hitter who had a little pop right-handed. His lifetime average was only .236, but he was far from an automatic out, especially in the clutch. He wasn't always a switch-hitter. When he came up to the Mets for 19 games in 1965, he hit right-handed exclusively and batted only .108 in 37 at-bats. That convinced him that he had to do something to improve his hitting, so he taught himself to hit left-handed and became a switch-hitter to take advantage of his speed coming out of the left-handed hitter's batter's box.

Two years later, as the Mets' regular shortstop, he played in 151 games and batted a respectable .254. He reinvented himself and became a guy who did all the little things that you don't necessarily see in the box score but that help a team win, bunt, hit and run, steal a base, work out a walk, move runners over, hit behind the runner. He was adept at all those skills. Whatever it took to help his team win, Buddy was going to do it.

There's a certain dedication that all good players must have if they are going to excel. If a player has that dedication, if he has the discipline for a long period of time, and if he doesn't give in to himself, a player can't help but improve and make himself valuable to his team. Some players, when you talk about them, you say, if this guy had given everything he had, he would have been better. You never had to say that about Bud Harrelson. He gave everything he had, every day.

Along the way, Harrelson tied a National League record for shortstops (since broken) by playing 54 consecutive errorless games in 1970, won a Gold Glove in 1971, made the All-Star team twice, played 12 errorless games in two World Series, and ranks second on the Mets all-time lists in games played and at-bats, third in triples, fifth in hits, seventh in stolen bases, and ninth in runs scored.

Don't be misled by Harrelson's size—or lack thereof. He was as tough as they come, which he proved in his defining moment as a player, Game 3 of the 1973 National League Championship Series against the Cincinnati Reds.

We had lost the first game in Cincinnati but won the second game 5-0 behind Jon Matlack's two-hitter. In the clubhouse after the second game, the writers asked Buddy what he thought of the Reds hitting against Matlack, and Buddy, with his typical impish, self-deprecating sense of humor, said, "They look like me hitting."

It was an offhand remark, not meant as a put-down, but the writers took it back to the Reds and they used it as a rallying cry against Buddy and the Mets.

Back in Shea Stadium for Game 3, Jerry Koosman started for us against lefthander Ross Grimsley, and we jumped out to an early lead. I hit a solo homer of Grimsley in the first inning and a three-run shot off another lefty, Tom Hall, in the second, and we were up 6-0 after two innings. My next time up, I was almost hit in the throat by Dave Tomlin, and I went to Kooz and begged him not to retaliate and hit one of their guys. I said, "Koozy, we've got a big lead. We got 'em. Don't give them anything to get excited about, please. I'm asking you, don't throw at anybody for me. You always protect everybody, but don't do it this time."

My plea fell on deaf ears. When Pete Rose came up, Koozy threw at him anyway. I was afraid that was going to start something, and it did.

By the fifth inning, we were ahead 9-2, and frustration was setting in on the Reds. The tension was palpable and you could almost sense there were going to be fireworks. With one out, Rose singled to center field, and when Joe Morgan followed with a ground ball to first and John Milner threw to Harrelson to start a double play, Rose slid into second base, hard like he always did, trying to break up the double play. The next thing you knew, Rose and Harrelson were rolling around on the ground, throwing punches at each other, and all hell broke loose.

Soon, it seemed as if the entire world was running to second base. I wondered what was going on. The dust started flying, the bullpens were emptying, and so I kind of jogged over to the group where players were scuffling all over the field with Pete and Buddy on the bottom of the pile. Harrelson was giving away about 35 pounds to Rose, but Buddy never backed off.

After he retired as a player, Harrelson returned to the Mets as a minor league manager and a major league coach. In 1990, when the Mets got off to a 20-22 start, Davey Johnson was fired with the team in fourth place. Harrelson took over and led the Mets to a record of 71–49 and finished in second place, four games behind the Pirates.

But the following year, the Mets slipped to fifth place and Buddy was fired.

His managerial experience was an unpleasant one for Harrelson, so he took the cure. He took off the uniform and moved up to the front office as part owner of the Long Island Ducks in the Independent Atlantic League where he could be the *firer* instead of the *firee.* That only proves that in addition to everything else he was and is, Bud Harrelson is smart.

Perhaps unfairly, because he was such an outstanding player for 16 major league seasons, the defining moment in Bud Harrelson's career, and the one moment for which he is best remembered, is his fight at second base with Pete Rose in Game 3 of the 1973 National League Championship Series.

It began in the previous game, after Jon Matlack had stymied the Cincinnati Reds with a 5–0 two-hitter to tie the series at one game each. After the game, sportswriters approached Harrelson at his locker.

BUD HARRELSON: My misfortune was that Matlack's locker was next to mine in Cincinnati. The writers were waiting for him to get off national TV, so I was sitting there and some writer—I don't even know who it was, all I heard was a voice—said, "What do you think about the Big Red Machine?"

And I said, "They looked like me hitting." It was all very innocent. I thought it was funny. The writers all laughed.

[Editor's note: Harrelson was well known around the Mets' clubhouse for his self-deprecating sense of humor. A case in point: recently commenting on the many injuries in baseball today and the number of players that land on the disabled list, Buddy said, "They don't make players like they used to. Today's players have too many muscles. Guys like me never pulled anything. I could have pulled a bone, but not a muscle."]

That's really all I said. I never said anything about Pete Rose, just the whole team. That they looked like me hitting. And they did. They couldn't hit—not that day they couldn't. This great team. The Big Red Machine!

I think it got twisted, because the next day Joe Morgan came out and grabbed me by the shirt and said, "If you ever say something like that about me again, I'll punch you out."

I can't speak for any of the Reds, and I don't know what was said to them by a writer or how my remark got twisted, but Morgan was obviously mad.

I said, "What?" I knew Joe. We grew up in the same area of northern California. Rusty was standing right there. He had played with Morgan in Houston, and Rusty said, "Joe, he didn't say anything about you."

Morgan said, "OK, I'm OK with it, but Pete's not. Pete's going to use it to fire up the team. He's going to come and get you. Pete will do anything to win."

TOM SEAVER: I was sitting on the bench, and you knew something was going to happen. You knew Rose was going to do something. You knew somehow, somewhere, Pete was going to do something because this was the Big Red Machine, and the most runs they scored in any one game in that series was two. Rose was totally frustrated, and you could see that.

I went to the clubhouse to get a cup of coffee, because it was cold. I opened the door, and the radio was on in the clubhouse and I heard, "...the fight...at second base." I was in the clubhouse, one foot in the door, and I turned around and ran down the runway under the stands toward the dugout. Concrete steps. And I was wearing spikes. And all of a sudden, my feet went out from under me and my head went down—ba-rump, ba-rump, ba-rump, ba-rump! I hit my head about four times.

I ran out there and my head was killing me. By the time I got out there, it was after the fact. It was all done, and I had the worst headache in the world. I was the one who got hurt the most (in the brawl), and I never got into it."

PETE ROSE: I gave him my little pop-up slide. Buddy says to me, "You blan-kety-blank," and I told him, "Hey, you don't know me well enough to say that." I grabbed him, and Wayne Garrett came tumbling into me from third base and all hell broke loose.

BUZZ CAPRA: The fight was my big claim to fame in the playoffs. I got more attention for that. I hadn't been in a ballgame for a couple of weeks.

We were shellacking the Reds pretty good, and Pete Rose, the aggressive player that he was, came into second base hard on Buddy, who was a New York favorite. Everybody loved Buddy. And of course the size factor (Rose was 5'11", 195 pounds and Harrelson was just 5'11" and 160 pounds), and there were some words said. Buddy got slammed to the ground, and here we go.

I was in the bullpen, and bullpen coach Joe Pignatano, leading the charge, opened up the bullpen gate. I was running out there—you got to be part of the team—but me and Buddy being the two smallest players on the team, I was hoping that I wouldn't get choked. But you got to go with your team, so whatever happens happens.

"There was a big pile-on at second base, and their pitchers were coming out of the bullpen, too. There was a lot of milling around, and just as things were about to come to an end, out of the corner of my eye, I saw something coming from the side. I saw an arm coming, and it punched me right in the ear. It was Pedro Borbón. I said it the next day, and I'll say it again. It was a cheap shot.

He apologized to me later on, but he punched me in the ear, and that's how far from the side he came. My hat came flying off. Duffy Dyer saw it and he grabbed Borbon, and I got some good shots in on Pedro. Then we were scuffling. There were bodies all over the place, and I fell to the ground and I was trying to cover up my head so I didn't get kicked. The next thing I knew there was somebody grabbing me by the back. It was Willie Mays. Of course, they didn't want to mess with Willie because they had a lot of respect for him.

I got up and my shirt was hanging out, and Willie and Rube Walker were holding me, and I wanted to get loose so I could get a few more shots at Borbón. I was infuriated. My hat came off, and Borbón, in a rage on his way back to the dugout, picked my hat up by mistake and put it on his head. One of his teammates pointed to the hat, and Pedro took it off his head, looked at it, and took a big bite out of it. Ripped it into three pieces. I still have that hat.

SPARKY ANDERSON: I think Pete was a little teed off about how things were going. I don't think Harrelson meant anything. It was a tough, hard slide, maybe a little harder than was necessary. I'm glad nothing really happened between those two, because of the size of them, that's not a fair fight.

It got ugly because a couple of guys did things they shouldn't have, and one of them was mine, Borbón. My God, you don't come in from the bullpen and coldcock somebody who's not looking at you. In all fairness, that wasn't done right. That poor guy [Capra]. I was right near it, and I heard the splat."

JACK LANG, New York *Daily News* writer: After the fight, the Reds were on the field and fans were throwing all kinds of garbage onto the field. Somebody threw a whiskey bottle out of the stands at Pete Rose standing in left field. It just missed his head. When that happened, Sparky Anderson took his team off the field, which he was justified in doing, and Chub Feeney, the National League president who was sitting near the Mets' dugout, asked Yogi to go out to talk to the fans.

They made an announcement on the public address system that if the fans didn't stop, the Mets would forfeit the game. So Yogi went out with Willie Mays, Tom Seaver, Rusty Staub, and Cleon Jones and they pleaded with the fans to stop or they'd lose the game."

BUD HARRELSON: Everybody in the world, when they hear Pete Rose or Bud Harrelson, that's what they remember. It wasn't as big a thing as it became. He used it, and we've talked about it. I did call him some names, and he said I didn't know him well enough to call him those names.

I talk to kids, and they'll say, "My dad tells me you had a fight with Pete Rose. Do you want to tell us about that?" I say, "Yeah, I hit him with my best punch," and everybody says "Yeahhh." And I say, "Yeah, I hit him in the fist with my eye."

That gets them off of it, because it wasn't a big thing. It was big in the sense that we were pitching and Pete was trying to get his team motivated. But the fight was nothing—but I didn't like what was going on. I got hit after the play was over.

I've always liked Pete. Right from the beginning, Pete and Tommy Helms were kind of mentors to me. When I first came up, they watched me, they saw my enthusiasm, they saw me struggle, and they encouraged me. They said relax, and they told me a couple of things to help me and I never forgot that.

"Pete and I did a card show together in 1995, and we signed those pictures. I signed a picture to him that said, "I'll never mess with the Hit Man again," and he signed one to me that said, "Thanks for making me famous."

Unless he gets a terrible injury, the only person that can stop **Jose Reyes** from being a superstar is Jose Reyes.

He comes with just about every talent you want—exceptional speed, an exceptional arm, and he's a switch-hitter who has some pop from both sides of the plate. I worry when he hits some home runs (19 in 2006) that he's going to start thinking about that and get away from the style of hitting that makes him great.

In a few years, Reyes has risen to the top among Mets shortstops (and they've had some very good ones) to where the only one I would rate above him at this time is Bud Harrelson because of his longevity, his body of work, and his championship pedigree. But it may not be long before Reyes soars ahead of even Harrelson.

Baseball is blessed right now with a group of incredibly talented young shortstops. There's Jimmy Rollins in Philadelphia, Hanley Ramirez in Florida, Troy Tulowitzki in Colorado, Stephen Drew in Arizona, J.J. Hardy in Milwaukee, Khalil Greene in San Diego, Ryan Theriot with the Cubs, Bobby Crosby in Oakland, Jhonny Peralta in Cleveland, and Michael Young in Texas, to go along with veterans Derek Jeter of the Yankees, Orlando Cabrera of the White Sox, Edgar Renteria in Detroit, Miguel Tejada in

Jose Reyes has the potential to be one of the best shortstops in the Mets', if not baseball's, history.

Houston, Rafael Furcal with the Dodgers, and Omar Vizquel in San Francisco.

Reyes can be as good as any of them, if he wants to be. It's all up to him. It's a matter of staying in shape, focusing on what he has to do on the field, and making sure that baseball always is his number one priority. If he does all that, Jose's future is beyond belief. But if the wrong things distract Jose, it can all go by the wayside. It's happened many times before, to a lot of players in many different sports. It's up to Reyes to be what he can be. He has the talent. He's an exciting son of a gun to watch. Man, oh man, he creates energy! To watch him run the bases is awesome.

Baseball is blessed right now with a group of incredibly talented young shortstops.... Reyes can be as good as any of them, if he wants to be.

Look at what he's accomplished already in only his first four full seasons: a .300 average in 2006, league leader in triples in three of his last four years, league leader in stolen bases in three straight years (2005–07), 840 hits, 486 runs scored, and 281 RBIs as a leadoff hitter. And he did all of this before he had even reached his 26th birthday.

What Reyes can accomplish in the game is unlimited, but, once again, I would caution that he must play hard, stay healthy, stay focused, and avoid off-the-field distractions.

Rey Ordonez was an amazing talent. He was a magician on the field with exceptional range and a great arm. He made some spectacular, acrobatic plays and won three Gold Gloves.

With all that, his career wasn't as good as it should have been. The problem with Rey was that he got a little involved in thinking he was more special than he was. I think he sometimes forgot that you have to bust it all the time. It may have been a lack of concentration or maybe that things just came too easy for him, but for a guy who had such talent and could make incredible plays, he made too many errors (27 in 1996, 102 in 963 major league games).

Ordonez hit a little bit from time to time, a lifetime .246 average, eight homers, and 260 RBIs in seven seasons with the Mets, but like so many guys who perceived themselves as big boppers but weren't, he kept flying out, flying out, flying out, and that's got to be frustrating for the hitting instructor. Ordonez was another guy who should have kept the ball out of the air but didn't.

Here I am dwelling on what Ordonez couldn't do, or what he should have done, and yet in almost a half century of Mets baseball, I've picked him third on my list of all-time Mets shortstops. It may be more of an indictment of the Mets than it is of Ordonez that, other than Bud Harrelson and who Jose Reyes can become, who else are you going to yell and scream about at short-stop for the Mets?

Rey Ordonez was a talented, exceptionally acrobatic shortstop, but he was plagued by too many fielding errors.

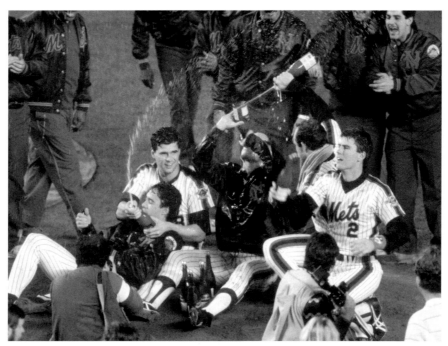

Kevin Elster (far right) celebrates the Mets' World Series victory with teammates. He would become the team's full-time shortstop in 1988. *Photo courtesy of Getty Images.*

Kevin Elster was only 23 in 1988 when he took over as shortstop for a very good Mets team that had Keith Hernandez, Gary Carter, Darryl Strawberry, Doc Gooden, and Ron Darling and had won the World Series just two years earlier. It was an enormous responsibility for a young shortstop, but Kevin handled it very well.

It wasn't until after he left the Mets and signed with the Texas Rangers as a free agent that Kevin made it big. He hit 24 home runs and drove in 99 runs in 1996. He had never come close to those numbers before and would never come close to them again, but that one year got him a big contract and set him up for life.

The numbers are not going to show it, but **Rafael Santana** did a great job for the Mets in the short time he was there. He may have batted only .218 in 1986, but he was the regular shortstop on a team that won the World Series.

Rafael Santana's seventh-inning single in Game 7 of the 1986 World Series was good for an RBI and kept the Mets rolling to an 8–5 victory. *Photo courtesy of Getty Images.*

Despite his problems at-bat, Santana had one big moment in Game 7 of the World Series, an RBI single in the Mets' winning three-run rally in the seventh inning.

Raffy fit in very well on that team, which didn't need his bat. What they needed from him was to make all the routine plays at shortstop, which he did, and to be consistent, which he was. He didn't have great speed or great range, but he made up for those inadequacies with a strong arm and with his knowledge of the opposition hitters. And he was a great teammate who was well liked by everybody.

Statistical Summaries

All statistics are for player's Mets career only.

HITTING

G = Games

H = Hits

HR = Home runs

RBI = Runs batted in

SB = Stolen bases

BA = Batting average

Shortstop	Years	G	H	HR	RBI	SB	BA
Bud Harrelson *First major league home run was inside the park at Pittsburgh's Forbes Field 8-17-67*	1965-77	1,322	1029	6	242	115	.234
Jose Reyes *Had three hits in four at-bats in 2007 All-Star Game*	2003-08	755	919	61	310	290	.287
Rey Ordonez *Played 101 consecutive errorless games from 1999-2000*	1996-2002	916	720	8	260	28	.245

continued	Years	G	H	HR	RBI	SB	BA
Kevin Elster	1986-92	537	355	34	174	10	.224
Had a three-homer game for Dodgers in the first-ever game at San Francisco's AT&T Park, 4/11/00							
Rafael Santana	1984-87	483	376	8	113	2	.248
Had an RBI single and later scored during seventh inning of Game 7 of 1986 World Series							

FIELDING

PO = Putouts

A = Assists

E = Errors

DP = Double plays

TC/G = Total chances divided by games played

FA = Fielding average

Shortstop	PO	A	E	DP	TC/G	FA
Bud Harrelson	2,246	3,710	183	686	4.8	.970
Jose Reyes	963	1,923	75	400	4.2	.975
Rey Ordonez	1,365	2,503	94	528	4.4	.976
Kevin Elster	767	1,380	62	214	4.2	.972
Rafael Santana	809	1,265	64	265	4.5	.970

FIVE

Third Baseman

It's only partly because third base had consistently been a problem area for the Mets that **David Wright** zoomed to the top of the list of all-time Mets third basemen in only four full seasons. The other part is that Wright is a special player.

Wright was taken by the Mets out of high school in the first round, the 38th pick overall in the 2001 amateur draft. He started his professional career with Kingsport in the Appalachian Rookie League and moved up the ladder to Capital City in the Class A South Atlantic League, St. Lucie in the Class A Florida State League, Binghamton in the class AA Eastern League, and Norfolk in the Class AAA International League. He burst onto the major league scene midway through the 2004 season. Only 21 at the time, he batted .293 with 14 home runs and 40 RBIs in 69 games and was an instant fan favorite, the big hope for the future.

In the next four seasons, Wright hit 116 homers, had 449 RBIs, and swatted batting averages of .306, .311, .325, and .302. He was the National League's starting third baseman in the 2006 and 2007 All-Star Games and

1.	DAVID WRIGHT
2.	HOWARD JOHNSON
3.	EDGARDO ALFONSO
4.	HUBIE BROOKS
5.	WAYNE GARRETT

David Wright became an instant fan favorite. In just four seasons, he's already reached all-time lists in most offensive categories.

won Gold Gloves in 2007 and 2008. He was a full-fledged star and the face of the franchise for the Mets.

Like Jose Reyes, David had not reached his 26th birthday and already he had moved up the ladder on the Mets all-time list in most offensive categories. He's fifth in homers, seventh in RBIs and second in batting average. In 2008, his 124 RBIs tied Mike Piazza for the Mets' single-season record.

In the decade or so before Wright arrived, Derek Jeter owned New York. He was the great young star in town, the idol of New York's young baseball fans, and especially young female fans. As Jeter has grown older and his time is passing him by, David Wright has replaced him—or is about to replace him—as the idol of young baseball fans and especially young female fans.

Wright is another guy who has an opportunity to be a Hall of Fame player. He has speed and he has power. The only time he gets in trouble is when he tries to pull the ball too much. He has awesome power the other way and is at his best when he hits the ball to right field and right-center.

David has an incredibly aggressive style of play. On defense, he will make an error from time to time, as anybody will. But he also makes unbelievable plays that you just don't see very often, and he has a strong and accurate throwing arm.

He's a star already, and if he continues to play as he has up to now, if he keeps getting better as he has every year, if he stays disciplined and doesn't let the off-field stuff interfere with what he's about in baseball, he has a chance to rank right up there with any third baseman—not just third basemen for the Mets—who ever played. It's up to him how good he can be.

So far, from what I have seen, that off-field stuff hasn't affected him. He seems to have his head on well enough to realize everything else has to be secondary and can't affect the number one thing in his professional life, to be the best player he can possibly be.

David appears to go about doing that very aggressively. He cares. You can see that this is somebody who has that crown waiting for him if he wants to take it, if he wants to discipline himself for a lot of years and be the kind of player that he could be. He and Jose Reyes are alike in that regard. They both have extraordinary talent. The Mets are fortunate to have these two young players on the left side of their infield who should be there for more than a decade, with All-Star teams and all the things that you look for in a

65

player. But those two guys have to remember it's about baseball, not the other stuff.

Don't get me wrong. I'm not saying there is a problem with either Reyes or Wright, but the landscape is littered with many who should have been Hall of Fame players. The sky was the limit for them, too, but unfortunately what happened off the field sometimes interfered and took them down. You have to be careful. There are examples in every organization, guys who should have been terrific stars for a long time letting off-the-field influences interfere with what they could have been.

Some Mets third basemen have played longer than Wright, a couple had big years, and a guy like Howard Johnson did some good things statistically. I love Howard. He's a great guy, and I will give him his due for what he accomplished. But let's face it; he's not like this kid Wright. This young man is it. In my opinion, he's the best third baseman the Mets have ever had. I think even Howard himself will agree with that.

Howard Johnson is a classic example of a baseball overachiever, someone whose career far exceeded most people's expectations, as he became one of the National League's most dangerous hitters in the late 1980s and one of the game's best switch-hitters ever.

Coming out of high school, Howard was just a mediocre prospect who was drafted in the 23rd round by the Yankees. When he failed to sign with them, it left him eligible for the secondary phase of the draft in January, and the Tigers, who valued him higher than the Yankees, made him their number one pick.

HoJo zipped through the Tigers' farm system and reached Detroit in 1982. The Tigers gave up on him after trying him at every position except pitcher, catcher, and second base. In three seasons, he appeared in only 197 games, hit 19 homers, and drove in 69 runs. Though he seemed to have arrived when he got into 116 games for the American League champion Tigers in 1984, batting .248 with 12 homers and 50 RBIs, the telltale sign of the Tigers' opinion came when he got only one pinch hit at-bat in the '84 World Series. That winter, the Tigers dealt him to the Mets in exchange for pitcher Walt Terrell.

At first, even the Mets didn't realize what they had. Howard started poorly and the Mets used him primarily as a backup third baseman to Ray Knight as well as shortstop and left field. Even in the championship season, 1986,

One of the best
switch-hitters ever to
play the game,
Howard Johnson is
also the nicest guy
you'll ever meet.
*Photo courtesy of
Getty Images.*

Knight was playing third base when it counted. I'm sure that hurt HoJo, but that's the way it was. Then the same thing happened to Johnson in the play-offs and the World Series with the Mets as happened to him with the Tigers—Howard was the forgotten man. He came to bat only twice without a hit in the NLCS and only five times without a hit in the World Series.

When Knight opted for free agency after the 1986 season, the Mets were left with little choice but to play Howard, and they turned the third base job over to him. Opportunity knocked for HoJo, and with it he flourished. He set a National League record for a switch-hitter with 36 homers, drove in 99 runs, and with Darryl Strawberry became the third 30-30 teammates (30 home runs and 30 steals in the same season) in league history.

His numbers in 1987 started HoJo on a spectacular five-year run during which he had 157 homers, 475 RBIs, made two All-Star teams, and led the National League in home runs and RBIs in 1991. He's third of all time in home runs by a Met with 192, third in RBIs with 629, third in stolen bases with 202, fourth in total bases with 1,823, second in extra-base hits with 424, second in doubles with 214, second in sacrifice flies with 50, and third in walks with 556.

Howard had such awesome power for a guy only 5'11" and about 180 pounds that Cardinals manager Whitey Herzog kept asking the umpires to check HoJo's bat for cork. The umpires kept checking but found nothing.... [He] suggested that Howard's arms should be checked instead of his bat.

Defensively, HoJo was adequate. He had limited range but a good arm and excellent reflexes that were better-suited for third base than shortstop. And he worked hard to improve.

Howard had such awesome power for a guy only 5'11" and about 180 pounds that Cardinals manager Whitey Herzog kept asking the umpires to check HoJo's bat for cork. The umpires kept checking but found nothing, and Herzog eventually accepted the fact that Howard's power was legitimate. Whitey even jokingly suggested that Howard's arms should be checked instead of his bat.

Howard's emergence as a star was perfect timing because it came just as players were beginning to get huge contracts. As a result, Howard signed some lucrative contracts and made big money. I couldn't be happier about that, because there isn't a nicer person in the world than Howard Johnson.

The Mets shuttled **Edgardo Alfonzo** between his natural position, second base, and third. He actually played more games for them at second than he did at third, but because there is such a dearth of good third basemen in Mets history, I'm putting Edgardo third on my all-time list of Mets third basemen.

Alfonzo did a very good job for the Mets in his relatively short time with them. They went to a World Series with him in 2000, and he had some extraordinarily big hits that year when he batted .324, belted 25 homers, and drove in 94 runs.

There was talk in the media that Alfonzo was older than he claimed to be. I have no clue if that was true. Be that as it may, he was a very productive player for the Mets.

Despite being shuttled between second and third base, Edgardo Alfonzo put up great hitting numbers during his stay on the Mets. *Photo courtesy of Getty Images.*

What I remember most about him in that 2000 season is that the Big Unit, Randy Johnson, couldn't beat the Mets, and one of the main reasons was Alfonzo. Pitching for the Arizona Diamondbacks that year, Johnson started three times against the Mets, and they pounded him all three times and won all three games. The first time, the Unit went 6⅓ innings and wasn't involved in the decision. In the next two games, the Mets knocked him out in the fourth and third innings. Alfonzo was five-for-eight against Johnson in those three games and 11-for-32 lifetime, a .344 average, with two home runs and five RBIs. That's not easy to do, because that big son of a gun had great stuff.

Alfonzo came out of Venezuela and was signed as an amateur free agent in 1991. The Mets liked him as a second baseman, and that's where he played in the minor leagues. But when Edgardo got to New York in 1995, Jeff Kent was playing second base, so the Mets moved Alfonzo to third.

The following year, the Mets switched Kent and Alfonzo. They obviously liked Alfonzo better at second than Kent, so they moved Jeff to third and put Edgardo at second, his natural position. It was Kent who was unhappy with the switch. He thought of himself as a second baseman, and he objected so strenuously to the switch that the Mets were eventually forced to trade him to Cleveland. In that trade, the Mets received a bona fide second baseman in Carlos Baerga, and that resulted in Alfonzo switching positions once more, back to third base. It was as a third baseman that Edgardo began to excel. He batted .315 in 1997 with 10 home runs and 72 RBIs and then followed that up with a .278 average in 1998 with 17 homers and 78 RBIs, again as the Mets' full-time third baseman.

When the Mets acquired Robin Ventura to play third base for a couple of years, Alfonzo moved back to second, and when Ventura left after the 2001 season, it was back to third for Edgardo, who must have felt like a Ping-Pong ball. But it didn't affect his hitting. He batted .308 with 16 homers and 56 RBIs.

Imagine if the Mets had left Kent at second and Alfonzo at third. They might have had both of them, two productive infielders, in the middle of their lineup for years. Who knows how things might have changed for the Mets?

For years, the "hot corner" was a "hot potato" for the Mets. Third base was a disaster area, a barren wasteland and a dumping ground for a cast of thousands in a seemingly endless search for someone who not only could play the position with skill, but who would also give the Mets some continuity.

In their first 25 years, the Mets employed 78 third basemen, a literal who's who, most of whom could effectively fall under the umbrella of Abbott & Costello's famed third baseman, "I Don't Know."

The cast of characters who played at least one game at third base for the Mets included major league managers Ken Boyer, Mike Cubbage, Jim Fregosi, Ron Gardenhire, Clint Hurdle, Ray Knight, Joe Torre, Bobby Valentine, and Don Zimmer, the first third baseman in Mets history.

The list also includes some who made their reputation at other positions, among them: Sandy Alomar, Wally Backman, Bobby Bonilla, Shawon Dunston, Jerry Grote, Jim Hickman, Ron Hunt, Jeff Kent, Dave Kingman, Phil Linz, Elliott Maddox, Amos Otis, John Stearns, and Frank Thomas.

It wasn't until the sixth year of their existence that the Mets had the same Opening Day third baseman for two consecutive years. Ken Boyer manned the position in the 1966–67 seasons and is among a collection of Mets third basemen who came to the team in the twilight of their distinguished careers and whose stays were too little and too late. As such, they fail to make the cut in selecting the top five third basemen in Mets history but are nonetheless important figures in the team's lore.

KEN BOYER: He had a near–Hall of Fame career. When he came to the Mets in 1966, he had spent 11 seasons with the St. Louis Cardinals, was an eight-time All-Star, had won five Gold Gloves, had batted over .300 five times, and had driven in 100 or more runs in two seasons.

He was captain of the great Cardinals teams of the 1960s and was named National League Most Valuable Player in 1964. He is one of three brothers to play major league baseball (along with Cloyd and Clete).

With the Mets he had 17 home runs and 74 RBI in 192 games before being traded to the Chicago White Sox midway through the 1967 season.

When he retired, Boyer had played 15 seasons, hit 282 home runs, driven in 1,141 runs, had a career batting average of .287, and had reached double figures in home runs in each of his first 12 seasons.

ED "THE GLIDER" CHARLES: Signed by the Boston Braves, he was blocked from making it to the major leagues by Hall of Famer Eddie Mathews. Charles spent eight years in the minor leagues in the segregated South; wrote and published poetry on such diverse subjects as the universe, racism, and baseball; and waited his turn. It finally came when he was traded to Kansas City and broke in with the Athletics as a 29-year-old rookie.

In a little over five seasons with the Athletics, he hit 65 home runs, drove in 319 runs, stole 73 bases, batted under .267 just once, and played an exceptional defensive third base.

Charles was traded to the Mets early in the 1967 season, took over at third base, and allowed the Mets to trade Ken Boyer. In New York, Charles became one of the Mets' most popular players. He was on the field at third base when the "Miracle Mets" clinched their first World Series title in 1969.

JOE TORRE: Born in Brooklyn, he returned home to New York when the Mets acquired him in a trade on October 13, 1974, at which point he had played 15 seasons with the Braves and Cardinals. The younger brother of Braves first baseman Frank Torre, Joe started his career as a catcher. He made the All-Star team six times as a catcher and three times as a third baseman.

In 1971, playing third base for the Cardinals, he won the National League batting title with a .363 average, led the league with 137 RBIs, and was named NL Most Valuable Player.

With the Mets, he batted .247 in 1975 and .306 in 1976. On July 21, 1975, he suffered his most embarrassing day in baseball when he hit into four double plays, each one following a single by Felix Millan. Later, he would blame his failure on Millan. "I never could have done it if Felix didn't keep getting on base," he quipped.

In 1977, the Mets made him player-manager. He retired as an active player midway through the '77 season with a career .297 average, 252 home runs, and 1,185 RBIs. He remained the manager of the Mets through 1981 without ever posting a winning record. Later, he managed the Braves and Cardinals before striking it rich as manager of the New York Yankees, with whom he won four World Series and made the playoffs in 12 consecutive seasons.

RICHIE HEBNER: "The Gravedigger" (he spent off-seasons digging graves at a Boston cemetery run by his father) hit 156 homers, drove in 615 runs, and twice batted over .300 in 10 seasons with the Pittsburgh Pirates and Philadelphia Phillies. He was traded to the Mets after the 1978 season, where he spent one season, batting .268, hitting 10 homers, and driving in 79 runs before he was traded to the Detroit Tigers.

RAY KNIGHT: He was sandwiched between two legends as third baseman for the Cincinnati Reds. In 1979, he took over the position from Pete Rose, who left Cincinnati to sign as a free agent with the Philadelphia Phillies. Three seasons later, Knight was traded to Houston to make room for Johnny Bench when the Reds switched Bench from catcher to third base to help extend his Hall of Fame career.

The Mets sent three minor leaguers to Houston on August 28, 1984, and brought in Knight to help solve their ongoing third-base problem. Knight started his Mets career poorly, batting .218 in 1985, but turned his career around the following season when he was named National League Comeback Player of the Year, batting .298, hitting 11 home runs, and driving in 76 runs while platooning at third base with Howard Johnson and helping the Mets win the pennant.

In the World Series against the Boston Red Sox, Knight batted .391, scored the winning run in Game 6 on the infamous ground ball by Mookie Wilson that scooted through Bill Buckner's legs, and hit the decisive home run in Game 7. For his efforts, Knight was named World Series MVP, but when a contract dispute with Mets management ensued, he opted for free agency and left the Mets for the Orioles. Knight's departure gave Howard Johnson the chance to blossom into a star as the Mets' full-time third baseman.

When his playing career ended, Knight had a short stint as manager of the Reds, worked as a television baseball analyst, and briefly served as a caddy for his wife, LPGA star Nancy Lopez.

ROBIN VENTURA: Free agency delivered Ventura to the Mets in 1999, after he had spent nine seasons as a star with the Chicago White Sox, where he had blasted 171 home runs, drove in 741 runs, and won five Gold Gloves.

In New York, he combined with Mike Piazza to give the Mets the most lethal one-two punch in their history. In 1999, Piazza and Ventura combined for 244 RBIs (Piazza's 124 is the best in Mets history, Ventura's 120 is third) as the Mets won 97 games (nine more than the previous season) and finished second in the National League East, and made the playoffs as a Wild Card.

Ventura's production declined in 2000 (24 homers, 84 RBIs), but he helped the Mets get to the World Series. When his production declined further in 2001 (21 homers and 61 RBIs), the Mets and Yankees got together for a rare trade in which the Mets got David Justice and sent Ventura to the Bronx.

Hubie Brooks had a world of talent and seemed to be on the fast track to becoming a star with the Mets at a time when they desperately needed one. The Mets were in the fourth year of what would be a seven-year drought—seven consecutive losing seasons—when Brooks arrived in 1980.

Hubie could run decently, he had a great arm, was a pretty good hitter, and showed occasional power in Shea, a ballpark that has never been known as a favorable park for power hitters. How great a prospect was Brooks? Out of high school, he was drafted in the 19th round of the June 1974 amateur draft by the Montreal Expos, but instead of signing with the Expos, he accepted a baseball scholarship from Arizona State, where he had such a successful college career.

He kept getting drafted…and kept refusing to sign. Four times from January 1976 to June 1977, he was drafted, each time in the first round—by the Kansas City Royals, Oakland Athletics, and twice by the Chicago White Sox. Finally, in the June 1978 draft, Hubie was again drafted in the first round, this time third overall, by the Mets. This time he signed.

Brooks made it to Shea Stadium in 1980 and appeared in 24 games for the Mets. The next year, he took over as their regular third baseman and held the position for four seasons. For the first time in their history, the Mets had stability at third base, historically their most troublesome position. Hubie batted .307 in 1981, but although his defensive play was good and his bat was

After a seemingly revolving door at the position, Hubie Brooks was the first third baseman to provide some much-needed stability.

adequate, he hit only 11 homers and drove in 136 runs in his first three full seasons. Hubie's offense perked up in 1984 with a .283 average, 16 homers, and 73 RBIs, but by then the Mets felt they needed more pop at a power position like third base than Brooks provided. They had acquired Ray Knight from Houston late in the 1984 season and moved Brooks to shortstop.

Mets fans liked Brooks for the way he played the game, but I think the Mets lost confidence in Hubie, who never became the player they thought he would be. In the end, Brooks' greatest contribution might have been in being the key man for the Expos in a trade that brought Gary Carter to the Mets. You have to give up something to get a talent like that, so Hubie was sacrificed to get Carter—and the Kid was the final piece to the puzzle that delivered the Mets' second world championship to Flushing.

If he did nothing else, **Wayne Garrett** would have earned a place in Mets history and in the hearts of Mets fans forever for one play in the stretch run of the 1973 pennant-winning season.

Garrett looked like a choirboy with his freckled face and flaming red hair (he might have been called "Rusty" by his teammates if that name wasn't already taken on the Mets), but he was a tough kid from Brooksville, Florida, whose brother Adrian also played in the major leagues. The Braves drafted Wayne out of high school, and the Mets picked him up in the Rule 5 draft of minor league players for $25,000, which some writers said was the best 25 grand the Mets ever spent.

Wayne was a good left-handed hitter, a gamer who did a terrific job for the Mets. In the 1969 championship year, it was Ed Charles, "the Glider," who played most of the time at third base. Garrett backed him up and platooned against right-handed pitchers. He worked hard and became a good third baseman, which was very important for a team that won primarily with great pitching and defense.

In the 1969 National League Championship Series against the Braves, Garrett batted .385 with a homer and three RBIs, and later in the 1973 World Series, he hit home runs against Catfish Hunter and Vida Blue.

A key figure in the Miracle Mets' playoff clinch, Wayne Garrett was the cutoff man between Cleon Jones and catcher Ron Hodges, firing a strike in time to tag out Richie Zisk in the top of the thirteenth inning. The Mets would go on to sweep the Pirates in the last series of the regular season and overtake first place in the division. *Photo courtesy of Getty Images.*

Garrett played eight seasons with the Mets, but longtime Mets fans will always remember him for that one play in 1973. It came on September 20 against the Pittsburgh Pirates.

To set the scene, the Mets had finished in third place in the National League East with 83 wins for three consecutive years, 1970–72, and had entered the 1973 season with high hopes. But we got off to a bad start, partly because we played poorly and partly because we had a lot of injuries, mostly in the first half of the season. Jerry Grote broke his arm and played in only 84 games. Buddy Harrelson was out with a variety of injuries and missed 55 games. Cleon Jones missed 69 games. I had undergone an operation on the hamate bone in my hand the year before, and although I played almost every game, it took a few months for me to regain the strength in my hand.

On August 5, we were in last place in the six-team National League East, 11½ games out of first. On August 14, we hit our low point with a record of 52–65. We were still in last place, but we had actually gained ground and were only 8½ games out of first.

That was the year Yogi made his famous remark, "It ain't over 'til it's over," and boy was he right. We started to get our injured players back one by one, and we began to win. We were fortunate that no other team was able to grab control of the division, and we slowly moved up in the standings.

On September 19, when the Pirates came to Shea Stadium for a three-game series, we had moved up to fourth place with a record of 74–77, but amazingly we were only 2½ games behind the first-place Pirates. We took the first game 7–3, and were only 1½ out. Then came Garrett's big moment in the second game of the series.

Jerry Koosman started for us against Jim Rooker. After eight innings, the score was tied 2–2. The Pirates scored a run in the top of the ninth, but in the bottom of the ninth, Duffy Dyer hit a two-out, pinch-hit, RBI double to tie it, 3–3.

In the top of the thirteenth, Richie Zisk singled with one out and, with two outs, a rookie named Dave Augustine hit a drive to left field that looked as if it would be a two-run homer. The ball hit right on the top of the left field fence, on the point of the fence, kind of like a "pointer" in stoopball. Now, 999 times out of 1,000, a ball that hits that point will bounce over the fence for a home run. Not this time. This was that one in 1,000. The ball bounced back toward the field, in play, and right into the hands of our left fielder Cleon Jones, who fired a strike to the cutoff man, Garrett, who turned quickly and fired a pea to home plate. Catcher Ron Hodges slapped the tag on Zisk for the final out of the inning.

(Editor's note: Augustine, who was credited with a double, had 29 at-bats in the big leagues, and that double was his only extra-base hit.)

In the bottom of the thirteenth, Hodges came up with one out and runners on first and second and lined a single that brought home the winning run in a 4–3 victory.

The newspapers the next day were hailing the play on Zisk by Jones, Garrett, and Hodges as evidence the baseball gods were looking down on the Mets. "Angels in the Outfield," one paper called it.

Now we were in second place, only a half-game behind the Pirates, and we had our ace, Tom Seaver, ready to start the final game of the series. The fans, who had begun to abandon the team and stay away from Shea Stadium, were suddenly excited again. There were 51,381 on hand for the game on September 21. Seaver was superb, holding the Pirates to five hits and striking out eight. John Milner, Garrett, and I each hit home runs, and we routed the Buccos 10–2 and miraculously took over first place in the NL East. I say "miraculously," because our record was only 77–77, the first time we had reached the .500 mark since May 29.

We would finish with a record of 82–79, the only team in the NL East with a winning record, and we won the division by 1½ games over the Cardinals.

Statistical Summaries

All statistics are for player's Mets career only.

HITTING

G = Games

H = Hits

HR = Home runs

RBI = Runs batted in

SB = Stolen bases

BA = Batting average

Third Baseman	Years	G	H	HR	RBI	SB	BA
David Wright *Through 2008 season, has a .367 career BA vs. Yankees*	2003-08	703	819	130	489	92	.309
Howard Johnson *Three-time member of the 30-HR, 30-SB club— 1987, 1989, 1991*	1985-93	1,154	997	192	629	202	.251
Edgardo Alfonzo *Went 6-for-6 with 3 HR, 6 runs scored, and 5 RBIs at Houston, 8-30-99*	1995-2002	1,086	1,136	120	538	45	.292

continued	Years	G	H	HR	RBI	SB	BA
Hubie Brooks *Wore uniform No. 62 in first four major league games, 1980*	1980-84, 91	654	640	44	269	31	.267
Wayne Garrett *Hit go-ahead HR in final game of 1969 NLCS vs. Braves*	1969-76	883	667	55	295	33	.237

FIELDING

PO = Putouts

A = Assists

E = Errors

DP = Double plays

TC/G = Total chances divided by games played

FA = Fielding average

Third Baseman	PO	A	E	DP	TC/G	FA
David Wright	468	1,375	91	108	2.8	.953
Howard Johnson	458	1,311	132	110	2.3	.931
Edgardo Alfonzo	351	956	42	85	2.6	.969
Hubie Brooks	356	969	90	80	2.7	.936
Wayne Garrett	495	1,362	91	139	2.7	.953

SIX

Left Fielder

I was talking with Tom Seaver one day, and **Cleon Jones'** name came up and—I'm paraphrasing him here—Tom said, "Cleon Jones could have been a Hall of Fame player. He had the talent to do it."

It comes down to what you want in your life.

Cleon, my word, he could run like a deer, he could flat-out hit, he had pop, he drove in runs. He didn't have a great arm, which may have been his only weakness.

You look back at some guys' careers and you say they could have done better. Jones is one of those guys. Don't get me wrong. Cleon had a good career, but he might have been something special if he had totally dedicated himself. I don't know what prevented him from reaching greater heights than he did. It's hard to under-

1.	CLEON JONES
2.	KEVIN McREYNOLDS
3.	CLIFF FLOYD
4.	GEORGE FOSTER
5.	BERNARD GILKEY

stand what makes some players tick. Sometimes a player gets comfortable in his role; he gets complacent in what he has accomplished, and he loses the hunger to do better.

It's tough to keep pushing all the time. Some guys do that and it makes up for a lot of their shortcomings. You have to push because the older you get,

Cleon Jones was a rarity for major league ballplayers: a left-handed thrower and a right-handed batter. *Photo courtesy of Getty Images.*

the harder you have to work. And I suspect Cleon didn't push hard enough or work hard enough. But man, could he hit!

He was a force in the championship year of 1969 when he batted .340, third in the league—to Pete Rose and Roberto Clemente, two all-time greats—a mark that stood for 30 years as the best single-season average for a Mets player until John Olerud hit .354 in 1999.

Cleon came out of Alabama, fertile ground for major league hitters (think Willie Mays, Henry Aaron, Willie McCovey, and Billy Williams). He was one of those rarities, a left-handed thrower and a right-handed hitter. There aren't many others like that who were successful major leaguers; Cleon and Rickey Henderson are two of the few.

Jones was in the center of two important moments in Mets history, one in the 1969 championship season, the other in the 1973 championship season.

On July 30, 1969, the Mets were in second place, five games behind the Cubs, when they faced the Houston Astros in a doubleheader at Shea

Stadium. In the first game of the doubleheader, the Astros scored 11 runs in the ninth inning and demolished the Mets 16–3.

In the second game, the Astros scored 10 runs in the third inning. In the midst of the rally, Houston catcher Johnny Edwards ripped a double to left field. On a field wet from an earlier rain, Jones was slow chasing down Edwards' double, and then he threw lackadaisically to the infield.

At that point, manager Gil Hodges left the dugout and walked slowly and deliberately out of the Mets' dugout and onto the field. At first it appeared he was heading to the mound to remove his pitcher. Instead, Hodges walked past the mound, past the shortstop and headed to left field where he confronted Cleon. Convinced Jones had not hustled after Edwards' hit, Hodges spoke briefly with his left fielder and then turned and, still moving slowly and deliberately, headed back to the dugout with Jones trailing behind him.

It was done quietly, but emphatically, and Hodges' action would speak volumes. It sent a message to Jones, the fans, and the rest of the Mets that Hodges would not tolerate a lack of effort from his players.

The incident seemed to galvanize the Mets who, after falling 10 games out of first place, rallied to overtake the Cubs to win their first National League pennant on their way to their first World Series championship. Jones was a key factor in the pennant run and in the postseason. He batted .429 in the National League Championship Series against the Braves and caught the final out of the World Series.

All of the Mets faithful have seen—over and over—the film of Jones catching the fly ball in Game 5 of the World Series off the bat of Davey Johnson and then genuflect to one knee in celebration of the Mets' first World Series victory.

Four years later, Jones was in the center of another important play in Mets history during the run at their second pennant. It came on September 20, 1973, in the thirteenth inning of a game against the Pirates. Dave Augustine hit a ball off the top of the left-field fence that bounced back onto the field, right into the glove of Cleon, who grabbed it and fired a strike to shortstop Wayne Garrett who, in turn, fired another strike to catcher Ron Hodges, who tagged Richie Zisk at the plate to end the inning. The Mets scored in the bottom of the thirteenth and went on to win the NL East title and the pennant.

The first left fielder in Mets history was Frank Thomas—no, not "the Big Hurt" but the man who came to be known by his teammates as the Mets' first bona fide power hitter.

Although he was not selected in the expansion draft, Thomas was an original Met and the team's left fielder and cleanup hitter in their first game, in St. Louis on April 11, 1962. (He was hitless in three official trips to the plate but drove in the second run in Mets history with a sacrifice fly in the second inning).

A native of Pittsburgh, Thomas signed with the home team Pirates out of high school. In 1953, his first full season with the Pirates, he belted 30 home runs and was being hailed as a successor to home-run king Ralph Kiner, who was traded away that June to the Cubs. In a touch of irony, Thomas and Kiner were reunited a decade later with the Mets, Kiner as a broadcaster, Thomas as their left fielder.

When the Mets obtained him from the Milwaukee Braves on November 28, 1961, for $125,000 and a player to be named later, Thomas had hit 223 home runs and driven in 746 runs for four teams.

Playing their home games in the Polo Grounds, the Mets sought a right-handed power hitter who could easily reach the inviting left-field seats (a mere 279 feet away from home plate), and Thomas, a dead pull hitter who crowded the plate, more than filled the bill.

In their inaugural season of 1962, Thomas was the Mets' best—and pretty much their only—power threat. He belted 34 home runs (no other Met hit more than 16) and knocked in 94 runs (no other Met drove in more than 59) for a team that had 139 homers and scored 617 runs all season. Thomas' 34 homers stood as the team record for 13 years; his 94 RBI remained a team record for eight years.

In his days as a Met, Thomas was known not only for his home-run power, but also for his quirkiness. On team charter flights, he would roll up his sleeves and pitch right in helping the stewardesses serve meals, and he loudly offered to bet all comers that he could catch any player's hardest throw barehanded. He had many takers, and he never lost a bet.

> Although he was well meaning, Thomas had a penchant for getting under the skin of opponents and teammates, including Mets manager Casey Stengel. While Thomas was adding to his home run total, Stengel preached that the Mets would be better served if Big Frank stopped swinging for the fences too often and tried spraying the ball to all fields.
>
> On the Polo Grounds' left-field fence was a banner for a clothing company, which advertised that the Mets batter who hit the sign most often during the 1962 season would be the lucky recipient of a boat. By the way he swung, Thomas made little secret of the fact that he was determined to win that boat. Stengel grew increasingly impatient watching Thomas try to pull every pitch to left field, and one day he could not resist chiding his cleanup hitter.
>
> "If you want to be a sailor," the old man said, "join the Navy."

I never knew what to make of **Kevin McReynolds**. He was Mr. Mellow. McReynolds was a mystery man. He would slip quietly into the clubhouse, go about his business, and slip out after the game before anyone noticed he was gone, behavior that didn't enamor him to a lot of baseball people. Some writers wondered if he even took a shower.

Some people thought McReynolds didn't care, but that was far from the truth. He played hard; he just looked like he didn't. He was one of those guys who just did not exude enthusiasm. There are players like that.

McReynolds also had a way of saying the wrong thing at the wrong time. I remember when the Mets played the Dodgers in the seventh game of the 1988 National League Championship Series and Kevin got in trouble because he said, "I can't lose. If we win, we go on to the World Series. If we lose, I'm going to be duck hunting in two days."

Even if you believe that, how could you say such a thing? I don't care if you think it, you can't say it. But that was Kevin. Some of the things he said would have been better left unsaid.

Baseball people used to talk about the "McReynolds patch." He stood in the same spot all the time, for every hitter. He wouldn't move. He'd wear that patch out. Davey Johnson's comment was, "You can't expect people to go outside of where they're comfortable," and McReynolds was comfortable in that patch.

I will say this, I never saw anybody better at cutting off balls hit down the left-field line and throwing the hitter out at second base. On that play, he's right there with any left fielder I've ever seen. He understood that play better than most. In 1988, he led the National League in outfield assists, which is rare for a left fielder.

Baseball people used to talk about the "McReynolds patch." He stood in the same spot all the time, for every hitter.

The bottom line is that Kevin McReynolds was a very good player who had some very good years, a lot of clutch hits, and an excellent career.

The talent was always there even if the enthusiasm seemed not to be. He was the first-round pick of the San Diego Padres, sixth in the country, in the June 1981 draft. He broke in with the Padres in 1983 and had a few very good years for a Padres team that went to the World Series in 1984. But the Padres must have thought that Kevin should have done more, because after his best year with them in 1986, they traded him. He was only 26 years old at the time, and he batted .288, hit 26 homers, and drove in 96 runs, yet the Padres included him in an eight-player deal with the Mets.

McReynolds had his best years with the Mets. In 1988, he set a major league record by stealing 21 bases without getting thrown out. The next

86

He sometimes got himself into trouble with the press, but it was hard to argue with Kevin McReynolds' play.

season, he extended that streak to 33 straight steals without getting caught. In five years with the Mets, from 1987 to 1991, after which he was traded to Kansas City for Bret Saberhagen, McReynolds hit 118 home runs and drove in 435 runs. He finished up his career with the Mets in 1994.

When his career was over, McReynolds, not surprisingly, seemed to drop out of sight. You don't hear anything about him. He doesn't work in baseball, he doesn't appear at card shows, he doesn't show up at reunions, he doesn't get his name in the paper. That's Kevin. The way he went about his job, his actions during his career, said something about how he felt about the game. It seemed as if it was never do or die for him. His attitude appeared to be "I have this talent, I'm going to play hard, I'm going to do what I can do, but when it's over, it's over."

A lot of people who have that demeanor use it as a defense mechanism, a safety valve not to appear weak, to just keep on an even keel. Everybody handles pressure in a different way. Apparently, the way Kevin handled it was to appear as if he wasn't interested in what he was doing, and if it worked for him, so be it. In my opinion, it worked for McReynolds. He was a very good player who had an excellent career, and you have to give him credit for what he accomplished.

Cliff Floyd's stay with the Mets was brief, just four seasons, but it was productive. He strikes out a lot like a lot of big hitters, but he has a great deal of talent. It's just a shame that he keeps getting hurt.

Floyd had been selected by Montreal in the first round, 14th in the country, in the June 1991 draft, and was traded to the Florida Marlins in the spring of 1997. With the Marlins, Floyd played on a World Series championship team and had some good years, including one huge year, in 2001, when he batted .317, hit 31 home runs, and drove in 103 runs.

That season helped Cliff get a big four-year, free-agent contract in 2003 for more than $26 million from the Mets. But Cliff's biggest problem in New York, and everywhere else, was that he couldn't stay healthy. It seemed as if every time he got it going, he got hurt. He had a weird accident where he hurt his arm; he had problems with his Achilles tendon.

He could hit and he was OK defensively, but he was so brittle that it was very difficult for him to get in the lineup consistently and to stay in the lineup when he did get in. He kept breaking down with injuries. In his first season

A talented outfielder who came to the Mets on a big contract from the Florida Marlins, Cliff Floyd was sidelined by too many injuries to play consistently. *Photo courtesy of Getty Images.*

with the Mets, 2003, he played in 108 games. The next year, he played in 113 games.

When he finally played a full season in 2005, he had a big year with 34 home runs, eighth best in the National League, and 98 RBIs. But the next year he was hurt again and played in only 97 games. When his contract ran out after that season, the Mets felt they couldn't re-sign him, so he signed as a free agent, first with the Cubs and then with the Tampa Bay Rays.

I like Cliff a lot, and not just as a player. Cliff Floyd is a good guy, a good teammate, and a positive presence in the clubhouse. He's a gamer who plays hard—when he's healthy. It's too bad he hasn't been able to stay healthy, but he had some good years and was able to get some excellent contracts. Good for him.

Obviously, **George Foster** had his greatest years with Cincinnati's Big Red Machine—and what years they were! He led the National League in RBIs for a major league record three straight years, 1976–78. He led the National League in home runs for two straight years, 1977 and '78. In 1977, he was voted the National League's Most Valuable Player when he led the league with 149 RBIs and 52 homers (at the time only the 10th player in major league history to hit 50 or more home runs in a season, the others being Roger Maris and Hall of Famers Babe Ruth, Hank Greenberg, Jimmie Foxx, Hack Wilson, Mickey Mantle, Ralph Kiner, Willie Mays, and Johnny Mize), and was fourth in the league with a batting average of .320.

Foster was drafted in 1968 by the Giants, who seemed to always come up with hitters, so much so that three years later they let Foster go in a trade to Cincinnati, where George became a star.

When the Mets had a chance to get Foster in a trade with the Reds after the 1981 season, their new owners, Fred Wilpon and Nelson Doubleday, supported the idea and showed their willingness to spend money to rebuild the Mets by approving a five-year contract for Foster worth $10 million, which, at the time, was one of the biggest contracts in baseball. That year Foster and Dave Kingman had each hit 22 home runs, Kingman for the Mets and Foster for the Reds, and had driven in 149 runs between them. The idea was to team Foster with Dave Kingman to give the Mets a powerful one-two home run tandem in the middle of the lineup that would help put fans in the seats.

While Kingman produced 37 homers and 99 RBIs for the Mets in 1982, Foster fell off from 22 homers to 13 and from 90 RBIs to 70.

Foster bounced back the following year to hit 28 homers and drive in 90 runs, his best season as a Met. Thereafter, he slowly declined. By 1986, at the age of 37, George had slipped to 13 homers, 38 RBIs, and a .227 average in 72 games when he was released in August, and the Mets went on to win the World Series without him.

Foster hooked on with the White Sox, but he got into only 15 games with the Sox, batted .216 with one homer and four RBIs and was released less than a month later.

Foster hit some home runs for the Mets, 99, and drove in 361 runs in five seasons. He never did even approximate his career numbers of 348 homers and 1,239 RBIs, mostly with the Reds, and you'd have to say his run with the Mets was disappointing. Because of what he had done in Cincinnati, and

George Foster put up his best numbers in Cincinnati, with the Big Red Machine of the 1970s. *Photo courtesy of Getty Images.*

because of the big contract, expectations were high for George in New York. Maybe the expectations were too high. He wasn't up to the caliber of play that he showed in Cincinnati, but in fairness to George, maybe the cast of characters in Cincinnati, surrounded as he was by all those great players like Johnny Bench, Tony Perez, Pete Rose, and Joe Morgan, made it easier for him than it was in New York where he didn't have a lot of great players around him. With the lineup we had in New York, there weren't as many opportunities for Foster to drive in runs as there were with the Big Red Machine.

Everybody talks about the problems the Mets have had at third base through the years, but the fact is that there are a few other positions where the Mets had even more problems, and left field is one of them. Left field has not been a strong position for the Mets. When you look at the Mets' left fielders you have to look hard to find five. So, despite what most Mets fans view as a disappointing stay by Foster, based on his stats he has to be included among the Mets' five best left fielders.

In 1996, his first season with the Mets, **Bernard Gilkey** had as good a season as any Mets left fielder ever had. He batted .317, eighth highest in the National League; hit 30 home runs; drove in 117 runs, eighth most in the league and fourth most in Mets history; and hit 44 doubles, fourth in the league and still the Mets' record. He also had 18 outfield assists.

Unfortunately, Gilkey never came close to those numbers again, and two years later, in July 1998, he was traded to the Arizona Diamondbacks.

Bernard Gilkey had one big season with the Mets, in 1996, but didn't come close to those numbers again.

Gilkey was a native of St. Louis who signed with the hometown Cardinals and had some decent seasons with them but never came close to the year he had with the Mets in '96.

The following year Gilkey fell off to 18 homers, 78 RBIs, and a .249 average; the year after that he was slipping even further when he was traded to Arizona in July.

Such is the state of left fielders in Mets history that just one super season was enough to get Gilkey on my all-time Mets team.

Statistical Summaries

All statistics are for player's Mets career only.

HITTING

G = Games

H = Hits

HR = Home runs

RBI = Runs batted in

SB = Stolen bases

BA = Batting average

Left Fielder	Years	G	H	HR	RBI	SB	BA
Cleon Jones *Finished 4th in NL Rookie of the Year voting in 1966, same year Tommie Agee won AL honor*	1963, 65-75	1,201	1,188	93	521	91	.281
Kevin McReynolds *Stole 21 bases without being caught in 1988*	1987-91, 94	787	791	122	456	67	.272
Cliff Floyd *Teamed with Carlos Beltran to each hit grand slams in the 6th inning at Wrigley Field, 7-16-06*	2003-06	468	440	81	273	32	.268

continued	Years	G	H	HR	RBI	SB	BA
George Foster *Led league in RBIs three straight seasons with the Reds, 1976-78*	1982-86	655	602	99	361	5	.252
Bernard Gilkey *Had 16 hits and 10 RBIs in his first eight games as a Met, April 1996*	1996-98	380	370	52	223	29	.273

FIELDING

PO = Putouts

A = Assists

E = Errors

DP = Double plays

TC/G = Total chances divided by games played

FA = Fielding average

Left Fielder	PO	A	E	DP	TC/G	FA
Cleon Jones	2,000	64	47	10	1.9	.978
Kevin McReynolds	1,454	60	23	11	2.0	.985
Cliff Floyd	754	31	11	5	1.8	.986
George Foster	1,177	40	28	11	2.0	.978
Bernard Gilkey	681	44	10	5	2.0	.986

SEVEN

Center Fielder

Carlos Beltran came to the Mets as a free agent in 2005 with a six-year contract worth $119 million that was a heavy burden for Carlos to carry. Could he be a $119 million player and live up to that contract? Most Mets fans will probably say he hasn't measured up to it. Well, who *can* measure up to a contract like that?

Beltran was drafted by the Kansas City Royals in 1995 and reached Kansas City in 1999, where he batted .293, hit 22 home runs, drove in 108 runs, and was named American League Rookie of the Year.

Five years later, with Beltran facing free agency, the Royals realized they would most likely be unable to sign him and sent him to Houston as part of a three-team trade. With the Astros, Beltran batted .258 in 90 games but hit 23 homers, drove in 53 runs, and helped the 'stros get to the playoffs.

1. Carlos Beltran

2. Mookie Wilson

3. Lee Mazzilli

4. Tommie Agee

5. Lenny Dykstra

It was during the 2004 postseason that Carlos blossomed. In 12 games during the division and championship series, he batted .435, tied Barry Bonds' record by hitting eight home runs in the postseason, and drove in 14 runs.

Carlos Beltran has already smashed a number of major league offensive records—and some of his best years are still in front of him.

That spectacular offensive explosion made Beltran the hottest property of the free-agent season and earned him that fat contract, with the Mets outbidding every other team. It also gave Mets fans high expectations that they were getting a player who would carry the team on his back—and his bat—to the Promised Land, just as he had carried the Astros to within an eyelash of the World Series. (They lost in the National League Championship Series to the Cardinals in seven games.)

When Beltran batted only .266 with 16 home runs and 78 RBIs in his first season with the Mets, there was much disappointment from Mets fans. But the simple fact is that a player doesn't become better just because you give him a lot of money, and the fans' expectations for Beltran may have been too much to ask.

Perhaps the fans in New York were spoiled, having seen center-field legends as Hall of Famers Joe DiMaggio, Mickey Mantle, Willie Mays, and Duke Snider. Carlos Beltran is no DiMaggio, Mantle, Mays, or Snider, but he is a darn good player whose numbers in four years with the Mets make him the best center fielder in their history.

In those four years, Beltran hit 117 home runs, drove in 418 runs, was named to the All-Star team three times, and won four Gold Gloves. He also cracked the Mets' top 10 lists in career home runs and RBIs. In 2006, Carlos broke the Mets' record for runs scored in a season with 127 and tied team records in home runs with 41 and in extra-base hits with 80.

In addition, Carlos is the only player in major league history to record four consecutive seasons (2001–04) of 20 or more home runs, 100 or more RBIs, 100 or more runs scored, and 30 or more stolen bases. And he is the major league's all-time leader in stolen-base percentage with a minimum of 200 steals (275 steals in 312 attempts for a percentage of .881).

All this and Carlos had just turned 31 at the start of the 2009 season. His prime years are still ahead of him, and there are still three years left on that big contract—still time to carry the Mets to the Promised Land and meet the high expectations of Mets fans.

For as long as baseball is played, **Mookie Wilson** (his real name is William Hayward Wilson, but he'll always be "Mookie" to Mets fans) will be remembered, and revered by Mets fans, for one at-bat in Game 6 of the 1986 World Series. It's one of the great moments not only in Mets history, but also in the history of baseball.

97

He'll always be remembered for the dribbler he hit through Bill Buckner's legs in Game 6 of the 1986 World Series, but Mookie Wilson was a solid-hitting outfielder, beloved by fans and teammates alike. *Photo courtesy of Getty Images.*

The Mets were down to the Boston Red Sox three games to two in the Series and trailing in Game 6 by a 5–3 score in the bottom of the tenth. When the bottom of the tenth started with the first two Mets being retired by Red Sox reliever Calvin Schiraldi (a former Met, to make it even more painful), it looked like curtains for the Mets. Shea Stadium was as quiet as a tomb as fans awaited the inevitable.

To make matters worse, as Gary Carter, the Mets' last hope, was batting, somebody in the press box inadvertently hit the wrong button, and flashing momentarily on Shea Stadium's giant message board were words congratulating the Red Sox on winning the World Series and Boston pitcher Bruce Hurst on being named the Series' Most Valuable Player. The words seemed to energize the Mets, and Carter hit a line-drive single to left field. The Mets' hopes were still alive.

Kevin Mitchell followed Carter with a pinch-hit single, and Ray Knight singled to center to score Carter and send Mitchell, the tying run, to third.

Mookie was the Mets' next batter, and he would have to hit against Boston's top reliever, Bob Stanley, who was brought in to replace Schiraldi. Mookie battled Stanley tooth and nail. With the count 2–2, Wilson fouled off two pitches, and then Stanley uncorked a wild pitch that went past catcher Rich Gedman to the backstop. Mitchell scored the tying run, and Knight carried the winning run to second base.

The count went to 3–2 and Mookie fouled off two more pitches. On the 10th pitch of the at-bat, Mookie hit a little four-hopper to first baseman Bill Buckner behind the bag. Buckner, suffering with a bad back and a bad ankle through the latter part of the season, reached down to pick up the ball, and it trickled through his legs as Knight scored the winning run, giving the Mets a 6–5 victory, tying the Series at three games each. The Mets would then win Game 7 and reign as World Series champions for the second time in franchise history.

Buckner would forever be remembered for his error, which is unfortunate because he was an excellent player who compiled 2,715 hits (one behind me on the all-time list) in an outstanding 22-year career.

And Mookie Wilson would forever be among the Mets' most revered heroes. Even if he had never hit that four-hopper to Buckner, Wilson would still be revered by Mets fans. He's one of their all-time favorites.

Mookie was a great Met. He was there a long, long time. He was a threat on the bases all of the time. Even though he struck out too much and walked too seldom for a leadoff man, he ignited the lineup. When Mookie was hot, the Mets did well. He was a key contributor to some great Mets teams. Fans loved him because he was always hustling. He created energy, and he was a very good guy on the ballclub. Everybody liked Mookie.

As he got older, Mookie began to break down physically. He never had a great arm to begin with, and surgery weakened it even more. Then he suffered a freak eye injury in spring training when a throw by shortstop Rafael Santana struck his glasses. Wilson was out for five weeks, and when he returned, his vision was affected and he had trouble judging fly balls.

Right up to his final game, Mookie always played hard, always ran every ball out, always hustled, and always had a smile on his face.

Eventually, Lenny Dykstra came along, and Mookie was reduced to a platoon player. Although he didn't like his reduced role, he continued to be a team player and leader until he was traded to the Toronto Blue Jays during the 1989 season.

When he left, Wilson was the Mets' all-time leader in stolen bases and triples and among the top 10 in total bases, extra-base hits, games played, at-bats, runs scored, hits, and doubles.

The trade to Toronto seemed to rejuvenate Mookie. After batting .205 with seven stolen bases in 11 attempts in 80 games for the Mets, he batted .298 and stole 12 bases in 13 attempts in 54 games and helped the Blue Jays win the American League East title. He even scored the run that clinched the division title for Toronto.

Right up to his final game, Mookie always played hard, always ran every ball out, always hustled, and always had a smile on his face. When his career was over, Mookie served as a coach for the Mets and later as a goodwill ambassador before slipping seamlessly into the role of elder statesman. He also experienced the thrill of watching his nephew and stepson, Preston Wilson, play eight games for the Mets in 1998 before being traded to the Florida Marlins as part of the deal that brought Mike Piazza to the Mets.

In the late '70s, the Mets were going through their worst stretch since their early years by finishing in last place three straight seasons. They were in dire need of a glamour boy, some young player with enough personality to put people in the seats and enough playing ability to give their fans hope for a better future.

Along came **Lee Mazzilli**, a home-grown local boy born and raised in Brooklyn, a switch-hitting center fielder with swarthy good looks who would become an immediate favorite with New York's vast Italian-American population.

The Mets made Mazzilli their first round pick, 14th overall, in the 1973 free agent draft. He rose rapidly up the ladder in the Mets' farm system and arrived

Maz had two tours of duty with the Mets before adjourning to their broadcast booth.

at Shea Stadium for 24 games in 1976. The following year he was the Mets' regular center fielder, batting .250 with six home runs and 46 runs batted in.

Maz had three more productive years before he started his decline. In 1978–80, he had 47 homers and 216 RBIs. His best year was 1979 when he batted .303, hit 15 homers, 34 doubles, scored 78 runs, drove in 79, had 34 steals, and strung together a 19-game hitting streak. He also was the Mets' only representative on the National League All-Star team and was the batting star in the NL's 7–6 win. Maz's pinch-hit home run tied the score in the eighth, and his bases-loaded walk scored the winning run in the ninth. He should have been the game's MVP, but it was instead awarded to Dave Parker, who had one hit and one RBI.

When Mazzilli's production fell off, the Mets traded him to Texas, just before the start of the 1982 season. But even then Lee helped the Mets, who dealt him for pitchers Ron Darling—who became a mainstay of their 1986 World Series championship team—and Walt Terrell, who would bring Howard Johnson to the Mets in a trade two years later.

Later, Maz was traded to the Yankees, then to the Pirates. When the Bucs released him in July 1986, the Mets signed him, and Maz returned to Shea, where he made important contributions to the Mets' second World Series championship as a part-time player and pinch-hitter.

In the World Series, Maz led off the eighth inning of Game 6 with a pinch-hit single and scored the tying run. In Game 7, he started a game-tying rally with a pinch-hit single off Bruce Hurst in the sixth inning.

In 1987, he led the National League with 17 pinch hits. But by the middle of the 1989 season he was waived by the Mets and picked up by Toronto, where he ended his career.

When his playing days were over, Mazzilli briefly tried his hand at acting, but eventually he returned to baseball. He managed in the Yankees' minor league system and later joined the Yankees as a coach, spending several years as bench coach to Joe Torre, who had been Lee's manager with the Mets.

When the Baltimore Orioles managing job opened, Maz got his shot as a major league manager in 2004. He improved the Orioles by seven games over the previous season and moved them up from fourth place in the American League East to third. But when the team regressed the following year, he was fired after 107 games, with the Orioles again in fourth place.

Eventually, Maz returned to the Mets a third time, but this time as a television analyst.

The center fielder and first batter ever for the Mets was Richie Ashburn who, on April 11, 1962, in front of a crowd of 16,147 in St. Louis, made the first out in Mets history when he flied out to Cardinals center fielder Curt Flood. In the bottom of the first, Flood returned the favor when he led off for the Cardinals and flied out to Mets centerfielder Ashburn, who recorded the first out in Mets history.

Ashburn played the final season of his career with the 1962 Mets and got 119 of his 2,574 hits (2,119 of them singles) as a Met. He led the '62 Mets in batting with a .306 average, hit seven of his career 29 home runs, and was the first Met named to the National League All-Star team.

Ashburn won two batting titles, finished second twice, led the National League in walks four times, led in hits three times, and was a five-time All-Star. He played 12 of his 15 seasons with the Philadelphia Phillies. When his playing career ended, he returned to Philadelphia and was an enormously popular broadcaster for the Phillies.

Ashburn was inducted to the Baseball Hall of Fame in 1995.

It hardly caused a ripple in the baseball waters when, on December 15, 1967, the Mets announced a four-for-two trade with the Chicago White Sox. Going to Chicago were Tommy Davis, a former two-time National League batting champion and a native New Yorker, born and raised in Brooklyn; Jack Fisher, a veteran right-handed pitcher who had gained notoriety by serving up Roger Maris' 60th home run in 1961 as a member of the Baltimore Orioles and by losing 24 games for the pitiful 1965 Mets; and two minor leaguers. Coming to the Mets were center fielder **Tommie Agee** and veteran utility infielder Al Weis.

Ostensibly, the deal boiled down to a swap of Davis for Agee. The White Sox hoped that Davis' still potent bat (he had batted .302 with 16 homers and 73 RBIs for the cellar-dwelling Mets that season) and veteran presence would help them contend in the American League. The Mets, who had finished in 10th place for the fifth time in their six-year existence, were trying to get younger and more athletic, with an eye to the future.

Tommie Agee's miraculous catch preserved a Mets lead and paved the way for their first-ever World Series victory.

Agee, a 25-year old Alabaman, had been originally signed by the Cleveland Indians and then traded to the White Sox in a deal that also sent Tommy John from Cleveland to Chicago. In 1966, Agee exploded on the scene by batting .273 with 22 home runs, 86 RBIs, and 44 stolen bases and was voted American League Rookie of the Year. But when he fell off to .234, 14–52 the following year, the White Sox deemed him expendable.

Agee arrived with the Mets in 1968, the same year as their new manager, Gil Hodges, who had spent the previous five years as manager of the Washington Senators. Hodges saw Agee as an upgrade in center field and a middle-of-the-order hitter, installing Agee in the number three slot in his

Mets batting order. But Agee was welcomed rudely, and painfully, to the Mets and the National League. In the first pitch he saw, in his first at-bat, in the first exhibition game, the newest Met was hit in the head by a pitch from Bob Gibson. Fortunately, his helmet saved him from serious injury, but he suffered a concussion and missed several days.

Perhaps it was the lingering aftereffects of the beaning, but Agee had a rough early go with the Mets. From April 15 to May 1, he was hitless in 34 consecutive at-bats, and by midseason, he was batting .174 with three home runs, 10 RBIs, and three stolen bases. When he broke his hitless streak with a single against the Phillies' Larry Jackson, Agee was accorded a derisive standing ovation from the sparse Shea Stadium crowd of 11,450.

Agee performed better in the second half of the season, but the final numbers were still horrid and disappointing—a .217 batting average, five home runs, 17 RBIs, and 13 stolen bases.

In 1969, Hodges moved Agee up to the leadoff spot in his batting order, a move designed to take some pressure off the young center fielder and, at the same time, give the Mets a hitter capable of starting a game with a home run.

Hodges' move proved to be a stroke of genius as Agee rebounded from his horrendous 1968 to bat .271, hit a career high 26 homers, drive in 76 runs and be a key figure in the Mets' remarkable, amazing, and astounding rise from ninth place in the National League to World Series champion.

Tommie was very strong, he ran the bases aggressively, and he played the outfield well. I was with the Montreal Expos in '69 and I remember playing a game at Shea, and Agee hit a ball into the upper deck that may have been the longest ball ever hit in Shea Stadium. It was the highest one for sure. I don't think anybody else ever did that. He hit it off Larry Jaster, and we couldn't believe it. Jaster had to live that down for years. And the Mets commemorated the shot by painting the seat where the ball landed, which remained a monument for 40 years until Shea Stadium was torn down after the 2008 season.

In the three-game sweep of the Atlanta Braves in the 1969 National League Championship Series, Agee batted .357 with two home runs and four RBIs. And in Game 3 of the World Series against the Baltimore Orioles, he led off the bottom of the first with a home run off Jim Palmer and made two spectacular catches that helped preserve the 5–0 victory and give the Mets a 2–1 lead in the Series.

In the fourth inning, with the Mets leading 3–0 the Orioles had runners on first and third with two outs when Elrod Hendricks hit a rocket to left center that had "double and two runs" written all over it. Agee seemed to outrun the ball and caught up with it just as ball and centerfielder were about to crash into the wall. As he reached up and speared the ball in the webbing of his glove, Agee crashed into the wall, still clutching the ball precariously in the webbing of his glove.

In the seventh inning, with the Mets leading 4–0 the Orioles loaded the bases with two outs when Paul Blair hit a drive deep to right center field. Agee took off at the crack of the bat and raced toward the fence. As the ball was about to land safely at the warning track, Agee laid out parallel to the ground and speared the ball just before it landed, skidding along the ground with the ball nestled safely in his glove. The Shea Stadium crowd of 56,355 gasped and then let out a mighty roar of relief and appreciation for Agee's second miracle, game-saving catch.

It was Tommie Agee's finest moment as a Met. He had two more productive seasons, but his numbers dropped off in 1972. After the season, he was traded to Houston, but he remains one of the true heroes of the Mets miracle season of '69, a big part of Mets history and a guy who deserves to be included among the top five center fielders in the history of the organization.

Lenny Dykstra had the best years of his career with the Philadelphia Phillies, but he had some good years with the Mets, too, and was a key player on the 1986 championship team.

Drafted by the Mets in 1981, Dykstra was a little guy, just 5'10" and 167 pounds, who could run, field, slap the ball around, and energize a team. He joined the Mets in 1985 and hit a home run in his second at-bat. Lenny had surprising power for his size. He didn't hit a lot of home runs, but he hit some of the biggest and most memorable homers in Mets history.

By 1986, the championship year, Dykstra saw more playing time when the regular center fielder, Mookie Wilson, suffered a shoulder injury and had begun his descent. At first, Lenny and Mookie were used as a platoon— Mookie, a switch-hitter, against lefthanders and Dykstra, a left-handed hitter, against righties. Dykstra was frustrated because he had to split time with Mookie, but when he got his chance, there was no better competitor and no harder player than Lenny Dykstra. He was a fan favorite because people saw him scuffling around, diving for balls, sliding into bases, and overall, just playing hard. The fans loved it.

Soon Dykstra, with a better on-base percentage than Mookie, was playing most of the time in center field. He combined with Wally Backman at the top of the batting order to ignite the Mets' offense. Together, Dykstra and

Called "Nails" because of his toughness, Lenny Dykstra was a key player in the Mets' '86 championship season.

Backman were called "Partners in Grime," befitting their style of play, a willingness to get their uniforms dirty. Lenny's nickname, "Nails," was evidence of the type of hard-nosed player he was.

Dykstra batted .295 in '86, hit eight homers, drove in 45 runs in the leadoff spot, and stole 31 bases. He followed that up by hitting .304 with a homer and three RBIs in the six-game National League Championship Series against Houston and .296 with two homers and three RBIs in the seven-game World Series against the Red Sox.

In Game 3 of the NLCS, his two-run homer in the ninth inning gave the Mets a 6–5 victory. In the pennant-clinching Game 6, he hit a pinch-hit triple in the ninth inning to jump-start a game-tying rally and then drove in the final run of a game-winning three-run rally in the sixteenth inning.

When the Mets lost the first two games of the World Series, Lenny led off Game 3 with a home run that started the Mets on their way to a 7–1 victory and their exciting comeback to win the World Series in seven games. In Game 4, he hit a two-run homer in the seventh inning that gave the Mets a 5–0 lead on their way to a 6–2 victory and a tie of the Series at two games apiece.

When Dykstra began to slide in 1989, the Mets traded him to the Phillies in a deal that was roundly criticized. The combination of the shock of being traded by the Mets and an injury may have caused Lenny to rededicate himself and become an even better player in Philadelphia than he was in New York. He pulled his rib cage and wanted to come back and play, but realizing he couldn't swing hard, he just tried to meet the ball and hit it all over the place instead of trying to hit home runs. He became a really good hitter then, because he realized the value of spraying the ball around and not over-swinging. In 1990, his first full season with the Phillies, he batted over .400 for a long stretch of the season and wound up hitting .325, the highest average of his career.

In 1993, having bulked up by some 25 pounds when he was still with the Mets, Dykstra had his biggest year as a member of the Phillies. He batted .305, hit 19 homers, drove in 66 runs, stole 37 bases, and was a major factor in the Phils getting to the World Series.

Dykstra was a big-game player. In 32 postseason games with the Mets and Phillies, he batted .321 (36 points higher than his career regular-season average), hit 10 home runs, and drove in 19 runs in 112 at-bats.

Statistical Summaries

All statistics are for player's Mets career only.

HITTING

G = Games

H = Hits

HR = Home runs

RBI = Runs batted in

SB = Stolen bases

BA = Batting average

Center Fielder	Years	G	H	HR	RBI	SB	BA
Carlos Beltran *.417 BA (5-12) in four career All-Star Games entering 2009*	2005-08	596	620	117	418	83	.275
Mookie Wilson *Had league-leading 638 at-bats in 1983*	1980-89	1,116	1,112	60	342	281	.276
Lee Mazzilli *Collected two pinch-hits in 1986 World Series, one left-handed and one right-handed*	1976-81, 86-89	979	796	68	353	152	.264

continued	Years	G	H	HR	RBI	SB	BA
Tommie Agee *Hit for the cycle vs.* *Cardinals, 7-6-70*	1968-72	661	632	82	265	92	.262
Lenny Dykstra *Homered in first major* *league game, at* *Cincinnati, 5-3-85*	1985-89	544	469	30	153	116	.278

FIELDING

PO = Putouts

A = Assists

E = Errors

DP = Double plays

TC/G = Total chances divided by games played

FA = Fielding average

Center Fielder	PO	A	E	DP	TC/G	FA
Carlos Beltran	1,542	32	14	10	2.7	.991
Mookie Wilson	2,532	45	52	18	2.5	.977
Lee Mazzilli	1,632	41	21	9	2.5	.988
Tommie Agee	1,462	30	40	6	2.2	.974
Lenny Dykstra	1,084	21	10	5	2.3	.991

EIGHT

Right Fielder

The mere mention of the name **Darryl Strawberry** conjures up so many thoughts and images.

This is a guy that had every tool there is to be a Hall of Fame player, and he was on the fast track to becoming just that. He was big and strong, 6'6", 200 pounds. He could run like a deer. He had a powerful throwing arm. And he had such a sweet left-handed swing that some people compared him to Ted Williams, which is the highest compliment you can pay a hitter.

He hit tremendous, majestic, tape-measure home runs to distances that few hitters could reach. He could have been one of the all-time greats, and that's the tragedy of Straw: what might have been. He had some hiccups off the field, and they cost him a chance to have an exalted position in the annals of the game.

1. DARRYL STRAWBERRY

2. BOBBY BONILLA

3. RON SWOBODA

4. ART SHAMSKY

5. JOEL YOUNGBLOOD

Life hasn't been easy for Straw, and when you think about him you can only shake your head and lament how his enormous talent was never used to its fullest.

Darryl Strawberry was an incredible talent, but off-the-field problems prevented him from reaching his full potential. *Photo courtesy of Getty Images.*

Despite that, when you examine what he did accomplish in his years as a Met, he's easily their number one right fielder and one of the two or three greatest position players in the team's history. He's their all-time leader in home runs with 252, in RBIs with 733, in extra-base hits with 469, in runs scored with 662, and in walks with 580. He's also second in total bases, third in slugging percentage, fourth in stolen bases, fifth in doubles, sixth in triples, seventh in hits, and ninth in on-base percentage.

Strawberry was such a tremendous prospect as a youngster at Los Angeles' Crenshaw High School (one of his high school teammates was future Cincinnati Reds star Eric Davis, another frightening prospect for Crenshaw opponents) that when Strawberry graduated in 1980, the Mets made him the number one pick in the country in the free-agent draft.

After only 312 minor league games, including 129 games at Class AA Jackson in the Texas League where he hit 34 homers and drove in 97 runs, Darryl arrived on the Mets in 1983 and as a 21-year-old rookie blasted 26 homers, drove in 74 runs, stole 19 bases in 122 games, and was voted National

League Rookie of the Year. He was on his way to greatness—and to Cooperstown.

Straw hit more than 20 homers and was in double figures in stolen bases in each of his first nine seasons, and three times he drove in more than 100 runs. He also made the All-Star team as a Met every year from 1984 through 1990.

In the Mets' championship season of 1986, Strawberry hit 27 home runs, drove in 93 runs, and stole 28 bases. The following year, he hit 39 homers, had 104 RBIs and stole 36 bases; the year after that he again hit 39 homers to lead the league, drove in 101, and stole 29. It was shortly thereafter that Straw's problems on and off the field began to surface.

Nearing free-agency status, Darryl began to talk about returning to Los Angeles to play for the Dodgers and expressed a desire to hook up again with Eric Davis, his high school teammate and close friend. When he became a free agent following the 1990 season, Straw did leave the Mets and signed with the Dodgers. The next year, the Dodgers obtained Davis in a trade with Cincinnati.

Back home in L.A., Strawberry reunited with Davis and was earning an annual salary of $3,800,000 that made him the highest-paid player in baseball. Darryl should have been sitting on top of the world. But after one good season with the Dodgers—28 homers, 99 RBIs, and an eighth straight All-Star selection—his life began to spin out of control. His problems with alcohol and drugs coupled with several physical ailments and caused his numbers to plummet. He spent time in the minor leagues before the Dodgers released him early in the 1994 season.

He signed on with the San Francisco Giants as a free agent, but he was suspended by the league for violation of the drug clause. The Giants released him after only 29 games.

Strawberry signed to play with an independent team in St. Paul, Minnesota, where he seemed to rediscover his batting stroke and attracted the attention of the Yankees, who gave him another chance by signing him as a free agent in June 1995.

Darryl had a brief revival with the Yankees, hitting 11 homers and driving in 36 runs in 63 games in 1996, 24 homers and 57 RBIs in 101 games in 1998, and he helped them win the World Series in '96 and '99. But by 2000, he was out of baseball.

His is one of the saddest stories in baseball history, a player who will be remembered not so much by what he accomplished—his enormous talent that produced tremendous, tape-measure home runs—but by the demons that prevented him from being all that he could be.

Older now and more mature, Darryl is back with the Mets as a television commentator. He seems to have his life back on track. I care about Straw a great deal, and I pray that he can find peace, happiness, and comfort in this second phase of his life.

Bobby Bonilla played all over the lot for the Mets, a little first base, a little third base, a little left field, and a little right field, but I'm putting him as the number two right fielder in Mets history partly because he put up some pretty good numbers, but mostly because right field is one of those positions where there hasn't been a whole lot of talent for the Mets over the years. Comparatively speaking, except for Darryl Strawberry, nobody else had the stats that Bonilla had with the Mets.

Everybody talks about how the Mets have had trouble at third base throughout their history, but there are a few other positions—and right field is one of them—where the pickings have been slim. There are no Roberto Clementes on the Mets' all-time roster.

The Pirates drafted Bonilla in 1981, but four years later they left him unprotected and the White Sox grabbed him in the Rule 5 draft. Bonilla got to the White Sox in 1986. The Pirates still had such a high regard for him that, after he had played just 75 games for the Sox, they reacquired him in a trade.

In Pittsburgh, Bobby, a powerful switch-hitter, became the big-time player the Bucs thought they were getting back in '81. Over the next five seasons, Bonilla hit 113 home runs and drove in 483 runs for the Pirates and made the All-Star team four times. His breakout year was 1990, when he batted .280, was sixth in the National League in home runs with 32, and was second in RBIs with 120. The timing was fortuitous for Bobby Bo, because it came one year before he was eligible for free agency.

When he became a free agent after the 1991 season, the Mets jumped in and signed the New York native to a five-year, $29 million deal. His 1992 salary of $6.1 million made him baseball's highest-paid player.

Although he put up good numbers for the Mets over the next 3½ seasons—91 homers and 277 RBIs—he never produced for the Mets

Bobby Bonilla slugged his way through 3½ seasons in his first tour with the Mets, but he never reached the huge numbers he put up in Pittsburgh. *Photo courtesy of Getty Images.*

commensurate with his salary, and he didn't turn the Mets into contenders as they had expected. With him, the Mets finished fifth, seventh, and third in the National League East. He was shipped to Baltimore midway through the 1995 season.

Not only was Bobby Bo's tenure with the Mets disappointing, but it was also filled with controversy. He feuded with a sportswriter over a book titled *The Worst Team Money Could Buy: The Collapse of the New York Mets*, and he once telephoned the press box from the dugout to complain about an official scorer's decision.

The Mets reacquired Bonilla from the Dodgers after the 1998 season, but by then Bobby was 36 years old and his best years were behind him. He batted only .160 with four homers and 18 RBIs in 60 games, and he clashed with manager Bobby Valentine over lack of playing time. Three months after the season, the Mets closed out the Bonilla chapter in their history by releasing him.

*M*odesty prevents Rusty Staub from including himself among the best right fielders the Mets have ever had, but there is no question he belongs, if not ahead of Darryl Strawberry, whose numbers with the Mets clearly entitle him to being number one at the position, then high on the list. Staub, who spent nine years in two tours with the Mets, four of them as their regular right fielder, must undoubtedly must be regarded no worse than the Mets' second-best right fielder ever.

A six-time All-Star, Staub had a distinguished, borderline Hall of Fame career that spanned 23 seasons (he is tied for 19th on the all-time list with such notables as Henry Aaron, Rogers Hornsby, Carl Yastrzemski, Brooks Robinson, and Greg Maddux) and 2,951 games (12th all-time) with 9,720 at bats (32nd all-time), 2,716 hits (five behind Lou Gehrig), 292 home runs, 1,466 RBIs, 1,255 bases on balls, 4,185 total bases, 119 sacrifice flies (tied for eighth all-time), and a batting average of .279.

Staub holds several baseball distinctions:

- He is the only player in baseball history to get 500 hits with four different teams: the Astros, Expos, Tigers, and Mets.
- He joined Ty Cobb as one of the only two players to hit a home run before his 20th birthday and after his 40th birthday.
- He was the first player to appear in 162 games in a season as a designated hitter (in 1978 with Detroit).

As a Met in 1975, Staub set a team record with 105 RBI that stood for 15 years and led the National League in both pinch-hits and pinch-hit RBIs in two consecutive seasons, 1983–84.

On the Mets' all-time list, Staub is second in pinch-hits with 77, second in pinch-hit home runs with six, 10th in on-base percentage with .358, and sixth in sacrifice flies with 37.

Asked about Staub, Yogi Berra, a man of few words who managed Rusty in the 1973 National League championship year, said, "He could hit."

Berra recalled that Staub belted three home runs and drove in five runs in the National League Championship Series against the Reds and made a game-saving catch on a drive by Dan Driessen with two runners on and two outs in the eleventh inning of Game 4. As he made the catch, Staub crashed into the right-field wall and banged up his right shoulder. The Reds won the game in the twelfth, and Staub was forced to sit out the fifth game, which the Mets won to clinch the pennant.

Staub missed the first game of the World Series against Oakland but returned for Game 2. He couldn't throw, but he could hit, and he led the Mets in batting for the Series with a .423 average. In Game 4, he had four hits in four at-bats and five RBI, including a three-run homer off Ken Holtzman.

Known affectionately as "Le Grand Orange" in Montreal, Staub's No. 10 jersey was the first uniform retired by the Expos. In 1986, he and Bud Harrelson were the first players inducted in the Mets Hall of Fame.

Here is how Staub is viewed by his peers:

GARY CARTER: Rusty had left Montreal when I got there, but he was an inspiration and a role model for me because he had been so highly regarded for his attempts at speaking French. He was the reason I took a Berlitz course in French so that I could fit in with the community.

My agent was Jerry Petrie, who had represented Rusty and the great hockey player Guy Lafleur. Jerry advised me to follow the lead of Rusty and Guy, which I did. At the time, I hadn't met Rusty. When I did meet him, I had the opportunity to tell him what a great influence he was on me.

Late in the 1979 season, Rusty came back to the Expos, and I had the pleasure of having him as my teammate. Then we were teammates again when I went to the Mets in 1985.

I think of Rusty as a big brother in baseball, someone who helped teach me to represent the game with the highest respect, which is what Rusty did.

BUD HARRELSON: Rusty was a smart player. He knew a lot about the game. If you wanted to listen, he had so much to offer—but he didn't offer it to everybody. If you wanted his help, he'd help you, but he never pushed himself on people.

He could play the game. He played hard, and he played hurt, and he's a good guy—the best. He's a people person. If he likes you, he'll do anything for you.

Like a lot of players, Rusty had a routine. When he came to the ballpark, he went into his routine, and you'd better not mess with it. One of the first things he did when he got to the clubhouse was go right to the trainer's room and get his ankles taped before every game. One day, a guy said, "Can you believe he gets his ankles taped every day and he can't run? Why does he get his ankles taped?"

And I said, "Maybe you should tape your ankles and you'd hit .300 too."

Rusty and I are like brothers. We got to be good friends when he came to the Mets in 1972. He took me out to dinner and we'd talk. He became my mentor. He watched out for me. We were together a lot. In 1980, my last year, I signed with the Texas Rangers and Rusty was there, so we were teammates again. And then after I retired, I returned to the Mets as a coach and Rusty came back as a player-coach, and we were together again. I couldn't get rid of him, and I still can't.

In his charity work today, his celebrities now are mostly all chefs. He does this big chef thing at the Alpine Country Club in New Jersey and he's The Man with these people. They all love him. There are some movie stars that come and TV people, and I'm the only former player who's invited and I go every year. It's a great thing that he does, and I'm very honored to be included.

We talk on the phone. He'll call me to see how I'm doing, or I'll call him to check in and I'll leave him a message. His birthday is April 1, and mine is June 6. He's April Fool's Day and I'm D-Day, so I'll call him and leave a message like, "Happy Birthday you old so-and-so" because he's two months older than me.

I try to stay in touch with him, but he travels so much, it's hard to keep up with him. He gives of himself. He's involved in so many things—and head-over-heels involved, not just, "OK, I'll show up." When he's into something, he does it full-tilt. He's a go-getter, and he should be proud of all the things he's done in his life.

I have a genuine love for Rusty Staub.

You can pretty much consider **Ron Swoboda** and **Art Shamsky** as one entry, A and B, and, in fact, they were just that in the 1969 championship season, employed as a right-field platoon by manager Gil Hodges: Swoboda for 78 games, Shamsky 63.

I'm tempted to rate them tied for the number three spot in right field, but I'll give the slight edge to Swoboda because he was a Met longer than Shamsky (six years to four) and had slightly better numbers (69 homers to Shamsky's 42 and 304 RBIs to Sham's 162).

In six seasons as a Met, Swoboda never hit 20 homers, never drove in 60 runs, never made the All-Star team, and batted higher than .242 just once. Yet he remains one of the most popular players in the team's history, mostly because he had his biggest days on the biggest stage, the Mets' first World Series championship in 1969, the "Miracle Year."

Rocky signed with the Mets out of high school and reached the big club two years later, a big, strong 20-year-old with power and potential who hit some prodigious home runs. Despite a .228 average, Swoboda belted 19 home runs that first year and drove in 50 runs in only 399 at-bats. The Mets were convinced they had a future star.

Swoboda never reached the lofty goals the Mets predicted for him (his best year as a Met was 1967, when he batted .281 with 13 homers and 53 RBIs) except when it counted most, four years later.

With the arrival of Shamsky, Swoboda was reduced to platoon status. While the Mets were astounding the baseball world in 1969 with their drive from ninth place to the franchise's first pennant, Swoboda had slipped to a .235 batting average with only nine home runs and 52 RBIs. But he drove in half of those runs during the last five weeks of the season while the Mets were surging to the division title, and on September 15, he hit a pair of two-run home runs to drive in all of the Mets' runs in a 4–3 defeat of Steve Carlton and the Cardinals on the night Carlton struck out 19 batters.

Swoboda never even left the bench in the Championship Series three-game sweep of the Atlanta Braves because the Braves started three right-handed pitchers, Phil Niekro, Ron Reed, and Pat Jarvis; Shamsky got the call from Hodges to start all three games.

Swoboda's time was to come in the World Series against Baltimore. Unlike the Braves, the Orioles had two left-handers, Mike Cuellar and Dave McNally, in their starting rotation. That gave Swoboda his chance to contribute, and he made his greatest contribution against Cuellar in Game 4 at Shea Stadium. After losing the first game of the Series, the Mets won the next two and were looking to put down the hammer at home.

Ron Swoboda's amazing catch was, in my opinion, the greatest play of the 1969 World Series.

Swoboda had three singles in Game 4, but his biggest contribution came with his glove. With Tom Seaver and the Mets clinging to a 1–0 lead, the Orioles rallied in the ninth when Frank Robinson singled with one out and Boog Powell followed with a single, sending Frank Robinson to third and bringing up Brooks Robinson.

Brooks lashed a line drive to right center where Swoboda took an ill-advised gamble. Instead of playing it safely, letting the tying run score and keeping the go-ahead run on second base, Swoboda daringly left his feet, sailed through the air, speared the ball, and landed on his face. It was déjà vu for the Orioles, who had been burned the previous day by two spectacular catches made by center fielder Tommie Agee. Now Swoboda had burned them again with what I thought was the greatest play of that World Series.

Frank Robinson scored the tying run to make it 1–1, but Swoboda's catch, which would endear him to Mets fans forever, prevented the Orioles from a big inning that might have turned the game, and the Series, in their favor.

The Mets scored a run in the bottom of the tenth for a 2–1 victory and a three games-to-one–lead in the Series and completed the "Miracle" the next day with a 5–3 victory. Swoboda started Game 5 against left-hander Dave McNally, but with the score tied at 3–3 in the eighth, McNally was replaced by right-hander Eddie Watt. Cleon Jones led off with a double, and Donn Clendenon grounded out. Swoboda was the next scheduled batter. Instead of removing him for a left-handed pinch-hitter, Hodges stayed with Swoboda and Rocky came through with a double that delivered the go-ahead run.

Swoboda played one more season with the Mets, and when his decline continued, he was traded to the Montreal Expos. But he had already done enough in one October to become a permanent part of the folklore of the Mets and an all-time Mets fan favorite.

Art Shamsky came up in 1965 and looked as if he would be another big-time hitter in a long line of big-time hitters for the Cincinnati Reds. In his second season, he hit 21 home runs and drove in 47 in 96 games, including a three-day stretch in August when he tied a major league record by hitting home runs in four consecutive at-bats. When he regressed the following year, the Reds, already stocked with outfielders who could hit, shipped him off to the Mets.

Art Shamsky was a solid right fielder and left-handed bat who platooned with righty Ron Swoboda to form an effective double threat to opposing pitchers. *Photo courtesy of Getty Images.*

With the Mets, Shamsky found his niche as a platoon player, mainly sharing right field with Ron Swoboda: left-hitting Shamsky against right-handed pitchers, right-hitting Swoboda against left-handed pitchers.

Shamsky did a terrific job for the Mets for a couple of years as a platoon player, which is not easy to do. Sham was a good player. He could hit. To be able to perform when you're not playing on a regular basis is not easy, but Sham and Rocky Swoboda did it very well.

In the championship season of 1969, the Mets got great production from their right field tandem, Shamsky and Swoboda combining for 23 homers (14 of the 23 for Shamsky in only 303 at-bats) and 99 RBIs (47 for Shamsky).

Shamsky and Swoboda's biggest contribution came in the postseason. With the Atlanta Braves starting three right-handers in the National League Championship Series, Shamsky got the bulk of the playing time in right field and was the Mets' leading hitter in their three-game sweep, batting a torrid .538 (7-for-13).

In the World Series, the Orioles used left-handers (Mike Cuellar and Dave McNally) to start four of the five games, which gave Swoboda his chance while Shamsky was hitless in six at-bats.

Shamsky followed up his good 1969 with another productive season in 1970, a .293 batting average, 11 homers, and 49 RBIs. The next season, however, plagued by a chronic bad back, he slipped to .185 with only five homers and 18 RBIs. When the season ended, he was packaged as part of an eight-player trade and sent to St. Louis. He was released before he even got to play a game for the Cardinals.

Shamsky had brief trials with the Cubs and Athletics, but his back problems prevented him from duplicating his success with the Mets and living up to his early potential.

For the number five right fielder in Mets history, I'm giving the nod to **Joel Youngblood** over others such as Gus Bell, Johnny Lewis, Xavier Nady, Shawn Green, Jeromy Burnitz, Endy Chavez, and Ryan Church, based mainly on longevity.

Joel Youngblood is the only player in major league history to get a hit for two separate teams on the same day.

Youngblood played parts of six seasons with the Mets after coming over from the Cardinals in a 1977 trade on the June 15 trading deadline. He had some pop in his bat for a guy who was only 180 pounds, and he hit 38 homers for the Mets, with a season-high of 16 in 1979. He also had 216 RBIs, with a high of 69 in 1980, and made the All-Star team in 1981. With the Mets, Youngblood batted consistently in the .250 to .270 range with a high of .350 in 1981, when injuries reduced him to just 41 games.

Defensively, Joel was a sure-handed outfielder with good speed and an excellent arm.

The Mets traded Youngblood to the Expos on August 4, 1982, a day in which he set a major league milestone that still stands today, as the only player to get hits for two different teams on the same day. That afternoon, with the Mets, he singled against the Cubs. After the game, the Mets announced that Youngblood had been traded to the Expos. He jumped on a plane immediately and flew to Philadelphia in time to hit a single for the Expos against the Phillies' Steve Carlton that night.

Statistical Summaries

All statistics are for player's Mets career only.

HITTING

G = Games

H = Hits

HR = Home runs

RBI = Runs batted in

SB = Stolen bases

BA = Batting average

Right Fielder	Years	G	H	HR	RBI	SB	BA
Darryl Strawberry *Had three-homer games as a Met (1985) and as a Yankee (1996)*	1983-90	1,109	1,025	252	733	191	.263
Bobby Bonilla *Hit home runs both left- and right-handed in the same game 6 times in his career*	1992-95, 99	515	481	95	295	8	.270
Ron Swoboda *Mets Opening Day first baseman in 1967*	1965-70	737	536	69	304	20	.242

continued	Years	G	H	HR	RBI	SB	BA
Art Shamsky *Homered in four consecutive at-bats for the Reds in August 1966*	1968-71	406	316	42	162	4	.266
Joel Youngblood *Played eight different positions (all except pitcher) during major league career*	1977-82	610	519	38	216	39	.274
Rusty Staub *Batted .341 with 4 home runs and 11 RBIs in 11 postseason games in 1973*	1972-75, 81-85	942	709	75	399	6	.276

FIELDING

PO = Putouts

A = Assists

E = Errors

DP = Double plays

TC/G = Total chances divided by games played

FA = Fielding average

Right Fielder	PO	A	E	DP	TC/G	FA
Darryl Strawberry	2,044	60	46	20	2.0	.979
Bobby Bonilla	446	20	9	2	1.7	.981
Ron Swoboda	1,020	46	32	7	1.7	.971
Art Shamsky	406	16	3	6	1.7	.993
Joel Youngblood	880	58	17	11	2.2	.982
Rusty Staub	980	57	20	14	1.9	.981

NINE

Right-Handed Pitcher

He is "Tom Terrific." He is "the Franchise." Of the almost 300 players and managers in the Baseball Hall of Fame in Cooperstown, he is the only one depicted on his plaque wearing the cap of the New York Mets. He is the Babe Ruth, Walter Johnson, Stan Musial, Ted Williams, and Sandy Koufax of the Mets, the greatest player in the almost half century of their existence. No other player is even close.

He's **George Thomas (Tom) Seaver**, a former National League Rookie of the Year, three-time Cy Young Award winner, 12-time All-Star, 311-game winner (18th on the all-time list), five-time 20-game winner and five-time strikeout leader. He's sixth all-time in strikeouts with 3,640 and tied with Nolan Ryan for seventh all-time in shutouts with 61. He pitched 231 complete games and had a winning percentage of .603.

1. TOM SEAVER

2. DWIGHT GOODEN

3. RON DARLING

4. DAVID CONE

5. BOBBY JONES

Most of that, but sadly not all of it, happened while he was a Met. The fact that Seaver even was a Met is the most fortunate (for Tom and the Mets) circumstance in the team's history.

Seaver had been selected in the June 1965 draft by the Dodgers out of the University of Southern California but declined their offer and remained in college. In a special January 1966 phase of the draft, Seaver was selected by the Atlanta Braves, who got Tom's name on a contract calling for a bonus of $50,000. The signing was voided when it was revealed that the contract violated a college rule, coming after Seaver's USC team had begun its season.

When Seaver's father, a prominent California businessman, threatened to sue major league baseball for denying his son the opportunity to begin his professional career, Commissioner William D. (Spike) Eckert declared Seaver a free agent eligible to sign with any team willing to match the Braves' offer. Only three clubs stepped forward: the Philadelphia Phillies, Cleveland Indians, and New York Mets.

To break the logjam, Eckert decreed that a special drawing would be held. The names of the three teams, written on a piece of paper, would be placed in a hat, and the lucky recipient would be the team whose name was drawn. And on April 2, 1966, Eckert stuck his hand in the hat of his assistant Joe Reichler and pulled out the paper on which was written, "New York Mets."

Seaver started his pro career with Jacksonville, the Mets' Class AAA farm team in the International League, where he was 12–12 with an earned-run average of 3.13. The following year he came up to the Mets and immediately became the ace of their staff with a record of 16–13—no other Mets pitcher had won more than nine games—and was voted National League Rookie of the Year. The next year, Seaver again won 16 games.

Then his career really took off. He won 25 games in 1969, the "Miracle Year," and won his first Cy Young award. He also pitched his first of five one-hitters with the Mets, narrowly losing his perfect game with one out in the ninth on a single by a rookie named Jimmy Qualls.

In 1970, he won 18 games and tied Steve Carlton's major league record of 19 strikeouts in a nine-inning game, against the Padres, striking out the last 10 batters, another record. He won 20 games in 1971 and 21 in 1972. In 1973, he won 19 games and his second Cy Young Award. In 1975, he won 22 games and won his third Cy Young Award. He also lost another no-hitter against the Cubs with two outs in the ninth on a single by another rookie, Joe Wallis.

Tom Seaver is the only player in the Hall of Fame depicted wearing a Mets cap. He is posing here with his three Cy Young Awards. *Photo courtesy of Getty Images.*

From 1967 to 1977, Seaver won 189 games for the Mets, accounting for 25 percent of the team's total wins. He pitched 166 complete games, tossed 42 shutouts, and struck out 2,406 batters in that span, all Mets records. That's why he was dubbed "the Franchise."

As an opponent, I had so much respect for Seaver. I knew he had a game plan at all times. I never saw any pitcher who, on days he did not have his best stuff, win as many ballgames as Seaver did. He did it on guile and by realizing, "I don't have my fastball today" or "I don't have my curveball today," it was just an off day, which we all have, whatever it was. He recognized it, made adjustments, and tried something different.

I can remember sitting in the dugout and saying, "Guys, he's going to throw a lot of breaking balls today. He's not popping the ball. I'm telling you, he's going to throw a lot of breaking balls in the next few innings. I don't know if he's going to get that fastball back, but look breaking ball."

Seaver had an uncanny ability to understand himself. He was methodical. He was prepared. And he just had great stuff. You face a guy and you study him, and you're looking for inconsistencies or consistencies in certain things he does with a particular pitch. He was tough. Occasionally, I'd get a little something off him, but for the most part he was tremendously disciplined. With the great stuff he had, he had an idea how to get you out, and he went about his business like a surgeon and got you. He could do it. He could do all of it.

I played for a long time, and I faced so many great pitchers, Hall of Fame pitchers, such as Sandy Koufax, Don Drysdale, Juan Marichal—and I want to be careful not to overlook any of the great pitchers I faced, but there's no question Seaver was in the top 10 of the pitchers I faced. I'd even put him in my top five.

Believe me, hitting against Seaver was no day at the beach. I'm not sure how I did against him. I got him a couple of times, and he got me. There were times when he made me tote that lumber back to the bench, and there were times I got some decent hits off him. (Editor's note: Staub faced Seaver 92 times, had 22 hits in 78 official at-bats, a .282 average that is three points above Staub's career average. He walked 14 times, struck out 14 times, hit five doubles, three home runs, and drove in eight runs.)

I'm not very good at remembering stuff like that, but Tom is, which is part of what made him such a great pitcher. He once told me, "One game, I decided I was going to throw you a change-up because I was ahead." I don't even remember this, but he told me he threw me a change-up, and he must have gotten it up because I hit it out of the park.

One incident I do remember. It was late in my career, 1979, when I was back in Montreal after spending 3½ seasons in Detroit. I was mostly pinch hitting for the Expos, but that night we were playing in Cincinnati, Seaver was pitching against us, and I got a rare start. Seaver had us shut out through the first six innings and had a 2–0 lead, but in the seventh I hit a two-run homer off the façade of the second deck in dead-center field to tie the score. The Reds scored a run in the bottom of the seventh and won the game 3–2 and Seaver got the win, but I cost him his shutout.

Joe Morgan and I were going to have dinner after the game, so when the game was over, I headed to the Reds' clubhouse and I ran into Tom's wife, Nancy. I went over to her, kissed her and said hello, and she said, "Did you have to?"

I said, "Trust me, I'm in more trouble than he is."

I'm pleased that I had the opportunity to be Seaver's teammate with the Mets, from 1972–75, and again in 1983. The shame of the Tom Seaver saga is the way he left the Mets. It was all because of two men—M. Donald Grant, the Mets' chairman of the board, who first called Tom "the Franchise" but who accused him of being greedy for demanding a contract of $250,000 and resented Seaver's activities with the player's union, and sportswriter Dick Young, who took Grant's side against Seaver in his columns in the *New York Daily News.*

On June 15, 1977, the trading deadline, the Mets did the unthinkable. They traded Tom "the Franchise" Seaver to the Cincinnati Reds for four players. Because the deal was announced after a night game in Atlanta, the media referred to it as "the Midnight Massacre."

It never should have happened. It was mean-spirited. It was vindictive. It was everything that is not supposed to happen to someone who was the face of the franchise. What it did was ruin something for the Mets—and it hurt Seaver. He's human, he can be hurt, and it hurt him.

In 5½ seasons with the Reds, Seaver won 75 games. To make matters worse for the Mets, who have never had a no-hitter in their history, Seaver pitched one for the Reds on June 16, 1978, a year and a day after the trade.

Tom did come back to the Mets under a different administration. On December 16, 1982, 5½ years after they got him, the Reds traded Tom back to the Mets. He was in the twilight of his career, but he won nine games, second-most on the team, led the Mets in shutouts with two, in ERA with 3.55, in innings with 231, and in strikeouts with 135, all for a bad last-place team. But when he was left exposed in the free agent compensation pool, the Mets lost him to the White Sox.

When he left the Mets the second time, Seaver had 273 wins. He would win his 300th game wearing the uniform of the Chicago White Sox. He did it on August 4, 1985, against the Yankees on Phil Rizzuto Day in Yankee Stadium.

As much as it hurt him to leave the Mets, Seaver did get to play with some great players, such as Johnny Bench, Pete Rose, Joe Morgan, Carlton Fisk, and Jim Rice, and with some good ballclubs, the Reds, the White Sox, and the Red Sox. But for Tom not to have played his entire career with the Mets is a shame because he was truly "the Franchise." He was everything that represented the Mets, and they blew it. He should have pitched his no-hitter in a Mets uniform, and he should have won his 300th game in a Mets uniform.

I can remember in 1986, when I was assistant to Mets GM Frank Cashen, we were playing the Boston Red Sox in the World Series, and there was Tom Seaver sitting in the Red Sox dugout. I couldn't help thinking at the time, "What's wrong with this picture?"

Yet, in the history of Seaver's life, other than his wife and his children, the New York Mets are the greatest thing that ever happened to him. What he accomplished with the Mets, being a part of everything he was with the Mets, was spectacular.

Today, Seaver is a country gentleman back home in northern California. He is a vintner. He is as disciplined in trying to learn about the vineyards and the wine-making techniques as he was in studying his delivery, his mechanics, and how to make the ball do what he wanted it to do as a pitcher. Everything he ever put into baseball he's putting into wine making and viticulture. His vineyard is gorgeous. It's so meticulously kept. I call him "the Hermit on the Mountain." It's tough to get the hermit off that mountain.

There's a similarity to the way he approached pitching and the way he approaches wine making. Every year he experiences something different. Every year you're learning something new; you have to start from scratch. The weather is going to be a different condition than it was the previous year. You have to figure out a way to react to it. It has a lot of the same kind of dynamics as baseball. You have to adapt. You have to study. I can promise you Seaver is doing that. I know a little something about wine, and I can tell you he's making a damn nice wine. But knowing Tom and the perfectionist he was as a pitcher, I wouldn't expect anything less.

Tom Seaver is one of 11 players and managers with ties to the Mets who have been elected to the Baseball Hall of Fame, but he is the only one who spent the majority of his career with the team and the only one who is depicted with a Mets cap on his plaque.

These are the other nine Hall of Famers with a Mets connection.

RICHIE ASHBURN: He spent 12 of his 15 major league seasons with the Philadelphia Phillies and his final season with the Mets in 1962, their first year, after being purchased from the Chicago Cubs. At age 35, he batted .306 for the Mets, two points below his career average, and was the first Met named to the All-Star team.

YOGI BERRA: Yogi joined the Mets as a player-coach in 1965 after a distinguished 19-year career as a player, coach, and manager with the New York Yankees. He played the final four games of his 2,120 game career and got the final two hits of his 2,150 major league hits as a Met before retiring as a player. He managed the Yankees to an American League pennant in 1964 and the Mets to a National League pennant in 1973.

GARY CARTER: After spending 11 seasons with the Montreal Expos, he was obtained by the Mets in a trade on December 10, 1984, and was instrumental in helping the Mets win their second World Series in 1986.

RALPH KINER: A seven-time National League home-run champion with the Pittsburgh Pirates in the '40s and '50s, he never played a game for the Mets, but he has been associated with them longer than anybody else. He has been with the Mets from day one as a member of their broadcast team, serving as play-by-play announcer, color analyst, and host of the enormously popular postgame show *Kiner's Korner*. He continues with them to this day as an occasional television analyst.

WILLIE MAYS: After playing 21 seasons with the Giants in New York and San Francisco, he returned to New York at age 41 when he was traded to the Mets on May 11, 1972. He played his final 135 games for the Mets, with whom he hit the last 14 of his 660 major league homers and helped the Mets win the National League pennant in 1973.

EDDIE MURRAY: Murray joined the Mets in 1992 as a free agent and played two seasons with them, hitting 43 of his career 504 home runs.

NOLAN RYAN: He was drafted by the Mets on June 8, 1965, and was a Met for five seasons, winning 29 games, pitching two shutouts, and striking out 493 batters. On December 10, 1971, he was traded to the California Angels in exchange for Jim Fregosi. He went on to pitch 22 more seasons for the Angels, Houston Astros, and Texas Rangers, winning 295 more games, striking out another 5,221 batters, and pitching 59 more shutouts and seven no-hitters.

DUKE SNIDER: The famed "Duke of Flatbush," an all-time Brooklyn Dodgers hero, returned to New York in 1963 at the age of 36 when he was purchased by the Mets from the Los Angeles Dodgers. With the Mets, he hit 14 of his 407 career home runs.

WARREN SPAHN: The winningest left-hander in major league history, he was purchased by the Mets in 1965 at age 44 after 20 years with the Braves in Boston and Milwaukee. With the Mets, he won four of his career total of 363 games.

CASEY STENGEL: After being "retired" as manager of the New York Yankees, for whom he had won 10 pennants and seven World Series in 12 years, he helped launch the expansion New York Mets in 1962, becoming the first manager in their franchise history at the age of 71.

I remember the first major league game **Doc Gooden** pitched. It was in Houston on April 7, 1984. He was just 19 years old, and he pitched five innings, gave up one run, struck out five, and got the win. Jesse Orosco saved it.

It was so exhilarating to realize what we had, how fortunate we were to have him as our selection and to have a chance for him to pitch for this organization. You could just see that he had it all. He seemed to go about his job really well. He worked hard. Everybody liked him. Sometimes a rookie comes in and he's a little too cocky, but Doc had none of that. I'd see that determination he had on the mound, and that big smile of his that was so welcoming. He was a joy to be around and his future was limitless.

You could just see that Doc Gooden had it all.

The Mets had drafted him out of Tampa's Hillsborough High School in the first round and fifth pick overall in the June 1982 free-agent draft. They sent him to Kingsport in the Appalachian Rookie League, where he won five games and lost four and then moved him up to Little Falls in the New York Penn League for two games. The next year, he went to Lynchburg in the Class A Carolina League and really opened some eyes by winning 19 games and losing only four, pitching six shutouts and striking out 300 batters in 191 innings.

It's a huge jump from Class A to the big leagues, but Doc made it seamlessly and spectacularly. In 1984, at age 19, he was 17–9 with a 2.60 ERA, three shutouts, and a league-leading 276 strikeouts in 218 innings. He made the All-Star team, pitching two scoreless innings, and was named National League Rookie of the Year.

Gooden's arrival coincided with Davey Johnson's first year as manager and ushered in a new era for the Mets. They improved by 22 games from the previous year, going from 68 wins and sixth place to 90 wins and a second-place finish. The future was very bright for Gooden and the Mets.

In 1985, Gooden had one of the greatest seasons any pitcher had ever produced in the history of baseball, a record of 24–4, an ERA of 1.53, 16 complete games, eight shutouts, and 268 strikeouts. He led the league in wins, ERA, complete games, and strikeouts and won the Cy Young Award.

The elation of watching someone on your team do this stuff was thrilling. Gooden dominated everything. His talent was awesome. There are very few pitchers who can affect the game like Doc did that year. People wanted to be there to see him pitch. It seemed that nothing could stop Gooden, and the Mets, from becoming a dominant force in the National League for the next 10 years or more.

Then came the decline. He slipped to 17 wins in 1986, the championship season, and to 15 in 1987, which began with Doc in rehab for substance abuse.

In 1985, Doc Gooden had one of the greatest seasons any pitcher had ever produced in the history of baseball, a record of 24–4, an ERA of 1.53, 16 complete games, eight shutouts, and 268 strikeouts. He led the league in wins, ERA, complete games, and strikeouts and won the Cy Young Award.

He rebounded to win 18 in 1988 but the next year suffered a shoulder injury and won only nine games.

Again, Gooden rebounded to win 19 games in 1990, but then the fall was precipitous. Just 13 wins in '91, 10 in '92, 12 in '93, and only three in '94, when Doc's drug problems were now out in the open.

When all that stuff happened, not only was it shocking, but you actually felt bad. You were hurt that someone who seemed so perfect and so good had a fault. We all have them, but his became too big a fault. I always hoped he could conquer it. I know he's had a few other problems, but I keep Doc in my prayers. I hope he gets his life in order and doesn't fall back into the pit.

I felt terrible when all that stuff went down. I liked Doc a lot, and I'm not in a select group. I'm in a big group, because I think everybody felt the same way about him. We were shocked. That's why we always say the things we say about young players. If they don't let the off-field stuff get to them, they will be great players. There are a lot of stories about young players who fell by the wayside, unfortunately. That off-field stuff can ruin your life, and when it happens to a good person and a great talent like Gooden, it's especially sad.

For Doc, the sky was the limit. When all the trouble started coming, it obviously affected his talent. He was able to pitch in the big leagues with the Yankees, Cleveland, Houston, Tampa Bay, and the Yankees again (he even pitched a no-hitter with the Yankees, another guy, like Seaver, who should have pitched his no-hitter in a Mets uniform), but never again was he the dominating pitcher who came up in 1984.

Ron Darling may have been the antithesis to Doc Gooden. Although not as talented as Gooden, he had the same work ethic, the same determination, and none of the demons that plagued Doc.

Right from the start, you could tell that Darling was a great athlete. He could run (the Mets often used him as a pinch-runner), he had a great arm, he could field (he won a Gold Glove in 1989), he swung the bat pretty well, he was smart (a Yale man), and he was a workhorse (in a 10-year period from 1983–93, he pitched in 331 games and started at least 30 games in a season eight times).

After he got his feet wet and realized what it took to win, he was ready to pitch. He had a game plan, and he did the little things to help himself become a good pitcher and have a very good career, such as field his position, run, and swing the bat. He was really good at helping himself in most of the facets of the game in addition to pitching.

At Yale, Ron had earned recognition and caught the eye of major league scouts when he hooked up against St. John's Frank Viola, a future American League Cy Young winner, in a famous NCAA playoff game. Darling took a no-hitter into the twelfth inning, an NCAA record for the longest no-hit game, but lost his no-hitter, and the game, when St. John's pushed across the only run in the twelfth.

The Texas Rangers made Darling their number one draft pick, ninth in the country, in the June 1981 free-agent draft. Ron never pitched for the Rangers but was instead sent to the Mets on April 1, 1982, in one of the best

137

Ron Darling was a hard worker who brought intelligence and composure to the mound. He works now as a part of the Mets' television broadcast team. *Photo courtesy of Getty Images.*

trades ever made by the Mets. They traded their poster boy, Lee Mazzilli, to Texas for Darling and another right-hander, Walt Terrell, who would later be traded to Detroit for Howard Johnson.

After appearing in five games for the Mets in 1983, Darling moved into the Mets' starting rotation and was in double figures in wins for six consecutive seasons, with a high of 17 in 1988. Although overshadowed by Doc Gooden, Darling was a big part of the reason the Mets became the team they were in that period and a key man in the 1986 championship season. He won 15 games and pitched effectively in the World Series against the Boston Red Sox. Despite holding the Sox to three hits in Game 1, he was the hard-luck 1–0 loser on an unearned run.

Darling came back to pitch seven shutout innings to win Game 4 and tie the Series at two games each.

After winning 17 games in 1988, Darling slipped to 14–14 the next year, and was 7–9 in 1990. He was 5–6 when the Mets sent him to Montreal in July 1991. He left with 99 wins as a Met, fourth on their all-time list. Two weeks after landing with the Expos, Ron was traded to Oakland, where he had a small resurgence, winning 15 games in 1992.

Eventually, Darling came back to the Mets as part of their broadcast team, a position he still holds. His work as a television analyst is just like his work as a pitcher. He's well prepared, and he brings to the booth the same intelligence and insight he had as a pitcher.

When you talk about great trades, you have to put the one that brought **David Cone** to the Mets high on the list.

The Kansas City Royals signed Coney in the June 1981 draft, and he spent five seasons in the minor leagues before finally making it to KC in 1986. He appeared in 11 games with no record and was traded to the Mets in the spring of 1987. In the trade, the Royals got catcher Ed Hearn.

Soon after he arrived in Kansas City, Hearn suffered a torn rotator cuff in his right arm. He would play only 13 games for the Royals and leave baseball at the age of 27. Cone, meanwhile, went on to win 194 major league games, the first 80 of them for the Mets.

Cone came to the Mets, and you started seeing the stuff he had and you said, "Wow! How did we get this young guy?" Once again the Mets had a young pitcher that created excitement. When you start getting those types of young pitchers, that's how you win.

Late in the 1992 season, the Mets were looking to upgrade their offense, so they put Cone in a package and sent him to Toronto to get Jeff Kent and Ryan Thompson.

If getting Cone was one of the best deals the Mets ever made, letting him go was among the worst. Although Kent was a good player for the Mets, he never did for them what they hoped he would. And as good as the first half of Cone's career was, the second was even better. That's a rare thing in sports—that the second 50 percent of your career is better than the first 50 percent—especially for a pitcher.

As Cone matured, he improved. He probably realized what he could do if he really applied himself a little more and he became more disciplined. Sometimes when you're young, you're a little more frivolous than you would

139

The trade for David Cone may have been one of the best in Mets history. He was sent to New York from Kansas City in exchange for catcher Ed Hearn, whose career would end with a torn rotator cuff after he had played only 13 games with the Royals. Cone, on the other hand, went on to become one of the best big-game pitchers in baseball.

be as you start getting older and you realize how important some of this stuff is. After he left the Mets, David won 114 games, and a Cy Young Award, and he won 20 games for the Yankees in 1998, 10 years after he had won 20 games for the Mets. The best compliment I can pay Coney is that if there was a big game, having the ball in his hand was just fine for everybody. If you had to win a game, you were happy he was on the mound.

As if to atone for the mistake of trading him away, when Coney became a free agent in 2003, the Mets brought him back 11 years after they had traded him. But by then he was 40 years old and on the way out. He won only one game for the Mets.

If it's any consolation to the Mets, it was the last of Coney's 194 major league wins.

To those who judge a pitcher strictly by the radar gun, **Bobby Jones** was not that impressive. But when you look at what he accomplished and you compare him with other right-handed Mets pitchers, you have to give him his due. He won 74 games for the Mets. Among right-handers, only the elite—Tom Seaver, Doc Gooden, Ron Darling, and David Cone—won more.,

Jones, like Seaver, was born in Fresno, California. He was drafted by the Mets in the first round of the 1991 draft, the team no doubt hoping they could catch lightning in a bottle a second time.

The Mets weren't a very good team when Jones reached Shea in 1993, but he was a big part of their rebuilding program that got them to the World Series in 2000 under Bobby Valentine.

Jonesy had a good idea what he was doing on the mound. He moved the ball around on hitters very well. Like most pitchers, especially those who don't throw very hard, when he had his control he was very effective. You can't put him in the same class with a lot of other pitchers when it came to stuff, but he learned to use the stuff he had. He became a good pitcher by relying on his good breaking ball and by throwing to spots.

In his first four full seasons with the Mets, Jonesy won 49 games with mediocre teams. There were other guys who were supposed to be the leaders of those teams, but Jones really was the leader. He made the All-Star team in 1997 when he led the Mets with 15 wins. He pitched the bottom of the eighth inning of the All-Star Game in Cleveland, gave up a single to Brady

Bobby Jones had impressive control and could move the ball around on batters.

Anderson, then got Nomar Garciaparra on a ground-out, and faced more than 1,200 worth of home runs in Ken Griffey Jr., and Mark McGwire, striking out both of them.

The highlight of Jones' career came in the fourth game of the Division Championship Series in 2000. Bobby pitched the first postseason, complete-game one-hitter in 33 years, giving up only a fifth-inning double to Jeff Kent. The Mets beat the Giants 4–0 and advanced to the National League Championship Series.

That game must have opened somebody's eyes, because the next year Bobby signed a lucrative free-agent contract with the San Diego Padres.

$\mathcal{T}$he Mets have had more than their share of outstanding right-handed pitchers, some homegrown, some acquired in trades, some signed as free agents, some taken in the expansion draft, and several who had their greatest years with other teams.

Roger Craig won 10 games for the 1962 expansion Mets, a team that won only 40 games. Later, he became a pitching coach for the Detroit Tigers and is credited with being the guru of the split-fingered fastball. He also managed the San Francisco Giants to a pennant.

Jay Hook was the winning pitcher in the first victory in Mets history.

Gary Gentry won 13 games for the Miracle Mets of 1969 and pitched 6⅔ shutout, three-hit innings in Game 3 of the World Series, a 5–0 victory over Hall of Famer Jim Palmer.

Pat Zachry, who came in the trade of Tom Seaver, won 41 games for the Mets in 5½ seasons.

Craig Swan won 14 games in 1979.

Rick Reed won 59 games in five years as a Met and was 11–5 in the National League championship year of 2000.

Bret Saberhagen was a two-time 20-game winner and a two-time Cy Young Award winner for the Kansas City Royals and had a 14–4 record for the 1994 Mets.

Pedro Martinez had a Hall of Fame career with the Boston Red Sox before coming to the Mets in 2005.

John Maine is a mainstay with the current Mets, and young Mike Pelfrey took a giant leap in 2008, showing the stuff the Mets saw when they drafted him in the first round, ninth in the country, in 2005. Both Maine and Pelfrey have a chance to someday crack the list of top five Mets right-handed pitchers.

And then there's Nolan Ryan.

To Mets fans the name conjures up thoughts of what might have been. Nolie was drafted by the Mets in 1965, incredibly in the 12th round. He would spend the first five years of his major league career as a Met, winning 29 games, pitching two shutouts, and striking out 493 batters. He would go on to play 22 more seasons with the Angels, Astros, and Rangers; win 295 more games; pitch 59 more shutouts; strike out 5,221 more batters; and pitch seven no-hitters.

What an amazing career he had! It's no wonder Mets fans still cringe when they think about the Mets trading him away.

Hindsight is great, but go back to 1972, when the Mets traded Ryan to the California Angels for Jim Fregosi. Here was Ryan, this young raw talent who wasn't in the Mets' starting rotation, wasn't going to be in their starting rotation, and was unhappy because he wasn't in the rotation.

It goes down as one of the worst trades in baseball history, but the Mets desperately needed a third baseman, and they figured Fregosi would be the man to plug that huge hole for years and Ryan was expendable. Fregosi gets a bad rap because he never was what the Mets thought he would be.

People forget how good a player Jim Fregosi was—so good that the Mets not only gave up Ryan to get him, but also three other young players. Fregosi had been a six-time All-Star, but as a shortstop. He was one of the elite shortstops in the American League, and the Mets put him at an unfamiliar position. And then in spring training, he was taking ground balls from Gil Hodges in practice, and a bad hop broke Fregosi's thumb. Jim, who was a gamer, came back too soon. His thumb wasn't fully healed. He had a terrible year for the Mets and Ryan went to a team that was not very good. The Angels gave him his chance to pitch every fourth day, and he struck out the world.

I loved being Fregosi's teammate and I felt bad that he always got that horrendous rap for that trade.

When his playing career was over, Jim became a terrific manager for the Angels, the White Sox, the Phillies, and the Blue Jays. He took the Angels to the playoffs, and he won a pennant with the Phillies.

I think the world of Jim Fregosi as a player, as a manager, and as a person. To me, he's more than merely "that guy who was traded for Nolan Ryan."

Statistical Summaries

All statistics are from player's Mets career only.

PITCHING

G = Games

W = Games won

L = Games lost

PCT = Winning percentage

SHO = Shutouts

SO = Strikeouts

ERA = Earned run average

Right-Handed Pitcher	Years	G	W	L	PCT	SHO	SO	ERA
Tom Seaver *Belted three home runs for the Mets in 1972, had 13 for his career*	1967-77, 83	401	198	124	.615	44	2,541	2.57
Doc Gooden *Lifetime record of 28-4 against the Cubs*	1984-94	305	157	85	.649	23	1,875	3.10
Ron Darling *Had double-digit victory with single-digit loss totals for five consecutive years, 1984-88*	1983-91	257	99	70	.586	10	1,148	3.50

continued	Years	G	W	L	PCT	SHO	SO	ERA
David Cone *Struck out the side on nine pitches in the fifth inning at Cincinnati, 8-30-91*	1987-92, 2003	187	81	51	.614	15	1,172	3.13
Bobby Jones *Entering 2009, last NL pitcher to lose 19 games, (2001 with Padres)*	1993-2000	193	74	56	.569	4	714	4.13

FIELDING

PO = Putouts

A = Assists

E = Errors

DP = Double plays

TC/G = Total chances divided by games played

FA = Fielding average

Right-Handed Pitcher	PO	A	E	DP	TC/G	FA
Tom Seaver	205	464	27	40	1.7	.961
Doc Gooden	191	328	32	28	1.8	.942
Ron Darling	130	292	29	30	1.8	.936
David Cone	101	116	12	4	1.2	.948
Bobby Jones	79	193	11	12	1.5	.961

TEN

Left-Handed Pitcher

There are certain pitchers whom their teammates always want on the mound in big games. In the late '60s and early '70s, the Mets were fortunate to have two: Tom Seaver and **Jerry Koosman**.

There's something special that develops among teammates, a certain camaraderie and trust for one another. The best way I can explain it is that when everything's on the line and your teammates think it's great that you're on the mound, you're *somebody*. The Mets had two somebodies, and they were fortunate to have them for a number of years. Seaver and Koosman! That was some combination. Wow!

When they added Jon Matlack, the Mets had a trio that was unbelievable. When you came into New York as a visiting player and you had to face

1.	Jerry Koosman
2.	Al Leiter
3.	Jon Matlack
4.	Sid Fernandez
5.	Bobby Ojeda

Seaver, Koosman, and Matlack, it could put you in a slump in a heartbeat. Guys would come into Shea Stadium hitting well with Seaver, Koosman, and Matlack lined up to pitch, and if those three had their stuff together, oh boy, those hitters were in big trouble.

Koosman didn't have a Hall of Fame career, but he had an excellent career. In his time, he was as good a big-game pitcher as there was. Kooz was 4–0 in the postseason.

Seaver and Koosman! That was some combination. Wow! When they added Jon Matlack, the Mets had a trio that was unbelievable.

In the 1969 World Series, Seaver was the losing pitcher in Game 1, the only game the Orioles won. Koosman was scheduled to pitch Game 2, which was a very big game. If the Mets lost that game and fell behind the Orioles two games to none, it could have put an end to their dream right there. But Kooz held the Orioles to two hits over 8⅔ innings and beat Dave McNally 2–1. Seaver won Game 4 2–1 and Koosman closed the deal by going all the way to win Game 5 5–3 and clinch the Mets' first World Series.

In the 1973 World Series against Oakland, Koosman combined with Tug McGraw on a three-hitter to win Game 5 2–0 and put the Mets up three games to two, but Oakland came back to win the final two games at home and deprived the Mets of their second World Series championship in five years.

The Mets signed Koosman as a free agent in 1964. Three years later, he came up at the end of the season and appeared in nine games, while Seaver was winning 16. The next year, Koosman's rookie season, Seaver was 16–12, and Kooz was 19–12. He set Mets records for wins, shutouts (with seven), and earned-run average with 2.08 and was second to Johnny Bench in the voting for National League Rookie of the Year.

By 1969, Seaver was a full-fledged star. He won 25 games and Koosman won 17, and those two were as much responsible as anybody for the Mets' miracle rise to their first pennant and world championship. They were both dealing, I can tell you that. They combined for 42 wins and 388 strikeouts, and there was a lot of lumber being carried back to the old dugout by opposing hitters, mine included.

One of the most important days in that miracle run came on September 12 in Pittsburgh. The Mets had pushed ahead of the Cubs by two games when they met the Pirates in a doubleheader in Forbes Field. Koosman pitched the first game, and Don Cardwell pitched the second. The Mets not only won both games 1–0, but Koosman and Cardwell drove in the winning runs in each game. I doubt if that had ever happened before—two pitchers, teammates,

Jerry Koosman (left) was the type of pitcher guys wanted on the mound in a big game. He's pictured here with another talented pitcher, future Hall of Famer Nolan Ryan. *Photo courtesy of Getty Images.*

winning both ends of a doubleheader by a 1–0 score and those pitchers driving in the winning run in each game. What made that even more surprising is that Kooz wasn't a very good hitter, only a .119 career batter.

Koosman won 20 games in 1976 (21–10), and the next year he had arm problems and lost 20 (8–20). In 1978, he fell to 3–15, and the Mets figured it was time to move on. They had traded Seaver midway in 1977, and now they were ready to trade Kooz, who had told the Mets he wanted to go home to Minnesota. The Mets accommodated him by trading him to the Twins in a deal that brought Jesse Orosco to New York. In his first season with the Twins, Koosman rebounded to win 20 games (20–13) for the second time in his career.

Kooz was the real deal as a pitcher and such a wonderful guy. The one thing about him today that stands out for me is that when we get together for Mets reunions and we start telling stories, as all ex-ballplayers do, there's nobody in the history of the world that's ever told a story like Koozy. He gets every story wrong, even though he's convinced he's right. He'll take a lie detector test to prove he's right, but believe me, every story he tells is wrong. Every one. He's something. But I love him. I do.

Al Leiter had terrific stuff, and he won more games for the Mets, 95, than any lefthander except for Jerry Koosman and Sid Fernandez.

If Leiter had possessed a little more control when he was with the Mets, it would have made him happier. It certainly would have made the Mets happier, and he would have won even more games than he did. He had days with the Mets, before pitch counts became scrutinized, when he would

Al Leiter was aggressive, threw hard, and was able to sustain big pitch counts. He was the Mets' ace during his tenure (1998-2004), going 95–67.

throw 140, 150, even 160 pitches in a game. He was big and strong, had a great arm, and was a bulldog on the mound. Even with his control problems, Leiter was the ace of the Mets' staff in the 1990s and early 2000s and was as much of a leader on those Mets teams as anybody.

By the time the Mets got him in 1998, Leiter had won 60 games and earned two World Series rings, one with the Toronto Blue Jays in 1993 (he won Game 1 in relief) and the other with the Florida Marlins in 1997 (he started Game 7 and pitched six innings but was not involved in the decision).

Leiter is a local boy from New Jersey who was drafted by the Yankees in the second round of the 1984 draft. He had all that talent and he could throw hard, but he was erratic with his control. After winning seven games and losing eight in three seasons, the Yankees apparently grew impatient with his lack of control and traded him to Toronto.

He signed with the Marlins as a free agent in 1996 and helped them win their first World Series. But after that championship year, the Marlins began dumping salaries and traded Leiter to the Mets, who were enjoying a resurgence under manager Bobby Valentine.

Leiter led the 2000 Mets with 16 wins and helped them win the National League pennant. He started Game 1 of the World Series against the Yankees, and he started and was the losing pitcher in Game 5.

Leiter became a free agent after the 2004 season. He returned to Florida where he won three games before being sent back where he started, to the Yankees. He won four games for the Yankees and then retired.

A pitcher who had a career earned-run average of 3.18 for 13 seasons and 361 games, who struck out 1,516 batters and walked 638 in 2,363 innings, and who pitched 97 complete games and 30 shutouts in 318 starts sounds as if he must have been an ace—maybe even a borderline Hall of Famer. But those are the numbers of a pitcher who had a losing record, 125–126, and only five winning seasons in those 13 years. His name is **Jon Matlack**.

I liked Matlack a lot. His fastball, his curveball, and his change-up were all outstanding. He had great stuff, he was a very determined young guy, and he won some big games for the Mets. He could really pitch. What he didn't have was a lot of luck.

There were the injuries: a fractured skull in 1973 when he was hit by a line drive off the bat of Marty Perez, elbow surgery in 1979, and chronic shoulder problems.

(Left to right) Jon Matlack, Jerry Koosman, and Tom Seaver were perhaps the Mets' most potent trio of pitchers.

152

And there was the lack of support from a Mets team that, for most of Matlack's years there, wasn't very good.

Despite that, Jon won 75 games for the Mets in the five seasons from 1972–76, and he's on the Mets' all-time top 10 list in starts, complete games, wins, innings, ERA, strikeouts, and shutouts.

Matlack was the Mets' first-round selection in the 1967 draft, the fourth pick in the country. He burst on the scene in 1972 with a 15–10 record, a 2.32 earned-run average, 169 strikeouts, and four shutouts—and he was voted Rookie of the Year in the National League.

When Matlack joined the Mets, he was helped a great deal by having Tom Seaver and Jerry Koosman—two of the best pitchers in Mets history—to learn from. That helped Matlack develop, improve, and mature as a pitcher. And the way he started out, Matlack looked as if he was going to be a great pitcher for the Mets for many years to come.

In 1973, Jon combined with Seaver and Koosman to give the Mets a formidable Big Three that brought them their second pennant. Matlack pitched a brilliant nine-strikeout two-hitter to beat the Reds 5–0 in Game 2 of the National League Championship Series and won Game 4 of the World Series against Oakland 6–1.

In 1974, he led the league in shutouts with seven and was third in ERA with 2.41. In 1975, he was the winning pitcher in the All-Star Game. In 1976, he had his best season with 17 wins and six shutouts.

After that, the injuries began to take their toll. In 1978, Jon went to the Texas Rangers as part of a complicated 10-man, four-team trade. I hooked up again with Matlack in Texas in 1980 when the Expos traded me to the Rangers. At the time of the trade, Matlack paid me one of the nicest compliments you can give a player. Apparently, after the trade was announced, Matlack was talking with some other Rangers players and they said, "That's great. Rusty can be a good guy for us coming off the bench and filling in at different positions."

I was told that Matlack said, "If you think this guy is coming here to ride the bench, you better give it another thought." (Editor's note: Matlack was right. Staub, age 36 at the time, played in 109 games for the Rangers, his playing time curtailed by a fractured ring finger and dislocated pinky on his left hand, which landed him on the disabled list for only the second time in a 23-year career. Still, he batted .300, hit nine home runs, and drove in 55 runs and was used in right field, left field, first base, and as a designated hitter.)

You won't find the name Alvin Neill Jackson listed among my top five Mets left-handers, although it probably should be. He is one of the most beloved figures in Mets history and a better pitcher than his record would indicate. Jackson's problem was simply a matter of bad timing.

He was signed by the Pittsburgh Pirates in 1955 and reached Pittsburgh four years later. Over the next three seasons, he appeared in 11 games for them, had a 1–0 record and was exposed to the draft that would stock the National League's two expansion franchises in Houston and New York.

The Mets selected him in the expansion draft, and he was the starting pitcher in their third game in their history. He also recorded the Mets third win, an eight-hit shutout of the Phillies and the first shutout ever by a Mets' pitcher. He would pitch three more shutouts that season and 10 in his first four Mets seasons.

Alvin was only 5'10" and 169 pounds, and his heart was at least that big. He lost 20 games in the Mets' first year, but as Roger Craig, who lost 24 games that year, said, "You have to be good to lose 20 games, because if you're not good, they'll stop giving you the ball."

The Mets gave Jackson the ball 150 times in their first four years and Al won 40 games for a team that won 194 games, so he accounted for 20 percent of his team's wins.

Alvin's greatest moment as a Met came in the final days of that torrid 1964 pennant race, when four teams battled for the pennant right down to the final weekend. The Mets went to St. Louis to face the Cardinals for the last three games of the season, with the Cards clinging to a half-game lead over Cincinnati.

On a Friday night, Jackson dealt the Cards' pennant hopes a severe blow when he beat Bob Gibson, 1–0. The Mets also won on Saturday, but the Cards won the Sunday game with Gibson coming in to relieve in the fifth inning and clinched the National League pennant.

So impressed with Jackson were the Cardinals that after the 1965 season they sent their long-time captain and star third baseman, Ken Boyer, to the Mets in a trade for Alvin. In his first year with the Cards, Jackson won 13 games.

Forget his record. Alvin was a little dynamo with an awkward delivery that made him difficult for left-handed hitters. He didn't have anything overpowering, but he could get you out.

I remember a game against the Cardinals in 1966, when I was with the Astros. It was the Sunday afternoon before the All-Star Game, and it might have been the hottest day I ever experienced on a baseball field. It was stifling. The Astros used five pitchers. Jackson started for the Cardinals and pitched 7⅓ innings. No pitcher should have been left on the mound that long in that kind of heat. That's the kind of fortitude Alvin had.

And he's one of the best people you'll ever meet. He was born on Christmas Day, and he's been a gift for anybody who has had the pleasure of knowing him. He's helped so many people in their careers, young people that he helped get their feet on the ground the right way. He's just a special person. To me, the name Alvin Jackson is synonymous with the New York Mets.

Mets fans will remember **Sid Fernandez** fondly as that hefty lefthander who wore No. 50 to honor his home state of Hawaii, the 50th state of the United States, and as a pitching mainstay who won 16 games in the championship season of 1986.

It was El Sid's performance in the World Series that helped inspire the Mets and enabled them to come from behind to win the Series. Davey Johnson had dropped Fernandez from the starting rotation for the Series and moved him to the bullpen because of Fenway Park's Green Monster and because the Red Sox had a lineup loaded with strong right-handed hitters, such as Jim Rice, Don Baylor, Dwight Evans, and Dave Henderson. In the seventh game, Sid replaced Ron Darling in the fourth inning after the Red Sox had broken out to a 3–0 lead. He proceeded to hold the Red Sox hitless for 2⅓ innings, striking out four, and give the Mets a chance to come back and tie the game with three runs in the bottom of the sixth, eventually winning 8–5 to capture the franchise's second World Series championship.

In the Series, Sid pitched 6⅔ innings in three games, allowed one run, and struck out 10.

The Dodgers drafted Sid in 1981 and had high hopes for him as a possible successor to Fernando Valenzuela after Fernandez threw two minor league no-hitters. Eventually, the Dodgers grew disenchanted with Sid, mainly

El Sid won 98 games with the Mets and was a key pitcher in the Mets' '86 World Series win.

because of his weight problems (he was listed at 6'1", 230 pounds, but nobody believed it).

With the Mets, Sid would win 98 games, fifth on their all-time list and second behind Jerry Koosman for a lefthander; strike out 1,449 batters, fourth on the Mets' all-time list; and pitch nine shutouts.

In 1985, he was only 9–9 despite 180 strikeouts in 170 innings and an ERA of 2.80, and in 1989 he was 14–5 and in one game struck out 16 Braves batters.

Fernandez didn't throw very hard—he rarely broke 90 miles an hour—but he got a busload of strikeouts. His delivery made his ball hard to pick up—he threw with a short-arm delivery and the ball came out of his body. He also threw with a differential in speeds between his fastball and his curve ball, which was a big, swooping slow one that he could consistently drop over for a strike. His delivery and the differential of speeds in his pitches had hitters off balance and often so messed up that good hitters looked foolish against him.

I enjoyed my time with Sid immensely. We used to kid around all the time. Would he have been a better pitcher if he had been in better shape? I can't answer that. I can say that his weight didn't affect his arm. In that respect he was like Mickey Lolich, David Wells, and C.C. Sabathia today.

The bottom line is that Sid was what he was. Overweight or not, he was one of the five best left-handed pitchers in the history of the Mets.

Little did the Boston Red Sox know on November 13, 1985, when they traded **Bobby Ojeda** to the Mets as part of an eight-player swap, that less than a year later that trade would come back to haunt them.

The Red Sox had signed Ojeda as a free agent, and he won 44 games for them in six seasons, including an American League–leading five shutouts in 1984. But the specter of Fenway Park's Green Monster, the cursed left-field wall, loomed as an albatross for Ojeda, a lefthander who didn't throw very hard, and prompted the Sox to ship him to New York.

The Mets and Red Sox both benefited from the trade immediately. The Red Sox got Calvin Schiraldi, a young, hard-throwing right-hander who would help bolster the Sox bullpen with four wins and nine saves as they surged to their first pennant in 11 years. And the Mets got Ojeda, who would be their best pitcher with a team-high 18 wins and a 2.57 earned-run average in their championship season.

Things looked bleak for the Mets when they lost the first two games of the 1986 World Series to the Red Sox at Shea Stadium. Down two games to none, the Mets had to go into the Red Sox's pit, Fenway Park, for the next three games.

To start Game 3, Davey Johnson took a calculated risk and gave the ball to Ojeda. Davey was banking on Ojeda's experience pitching in Fenway Park and that the incentive of facing his old team would pump him up—and he was right. Bobby pitched seven solid innings in a 7–1 victory, and the Mets were on their way.

Ojeda also got the start in the famous Game 6, the Mookie Wilson–Bill Buckner game. This time he pitched six solid innings. He left the game with the score tied 2–2 and was not involved in the decision, but he had done his job. He silenced the powerful Red Sox bats and gave his team a chance to win.

Bobby Ojeda shows off his grip to reporters in November 1988; he severed the tip of his middle finger with a pair of hedge clippers earlier that year.

Bobby was another guy who got a lot out of his talent. He knew how to win. He had a great curveball, slider, and change-up. He threw from the side and was tough on left-handed hitters. He was savvy, and he was aggressive.

Ojeda wasn't afraid to pitch inside, which I believe to be the key to success in the big leagues. I don't mean hitting people. I mean pitching inside. Moving hitters off the plate. Getting them to look inside, thereby opening up the outside part of the plate and making hitters vulnerable to the pitch on the outer half.

A pitcher—especially one like Ojeda, who wasn't a hard thrower—has to pitch inside to be effective. Ojeda knew he couldn't overmatch hitters. He knew he had to pitch inside, and he did.

To me, the real measure of Bobby Ojeda, his guts and his determination, came in 1989. With three weeks left in the '88 season, Bobby suffered a horrendous injury. While trimming some hedges in his yard at home, he severed the middle fingertip on his left hand, his throwing hand. He came back the next season and won 13 games. Just having the courage to come back from what appeared to be a career-ending injury shows you his mental strength and tenacity. Bobby found a way to come back and pitch in the big leagues— not only pitch, but win.

The Mets have had other lefthanders who deserve mention, although they didn't make my top five list, such as Hall of Famer Warren Spahn, who won four of his 363 games with the Mets at age 44; Randy Jones, who won eight games for the Mets after he had two 20-win seasons and won a Cy Young Award with the San Diego Padres; Frank Viola, who won 20 games for the Mets in 1990, two years after he won a Cy Young award with the Minnesota Twins; Tom Glavine, who won 61 games in five years with the Mets, including his 300th major league victory; Oliver Perez, who has a chance to be one of the best lefthanders the Mets have had; Johan Santana, who is signed with the Mets through 2014 and is destined to leave them with some eye-popping numbers and certain to move into the elite top five left-handers in Mets' history.

Statistical Summaries

All statistics are from player's Mets career only.

PITCHING

G = Games

W = Games won

L = Games lost

PCT = Winning percentage

SHO = Shutouts

SO = Strikeouts

ERA = Earned run average

Left-Handed Pitcher	Years	G	W	L	PCT	SHO	SO	ERA
Jerry Koosman *Earned save in the 1968 All-Star Game as a rookie by fanning Carl Yastrzemski*	1967-78	376	140	137	.505	26	1,799	3.09
Al Leiter *Held Albert Pujols to an .091 average (1-for-11)*	1998-2004	213	95	67	.586	7	1,106	3.42
Jon Matlack *Only Met to lead NL twice in shutouts (1974, 1976)*	1971-77	203	82	81	.503	26	1,023	3.03

continued	Years	G	W	L	PCT	SHO	SO	ERA
Sid Fernandez *Allowed fewer than 7 hits per 9 innings during his career, 3rd best mark among all pitchers*	1984-93	255	98	78	.557	9	1,449	3.14
Bobby Ojeda *Had a 5-0 record against the Dodgers with a 1.85 ERA before the Mets traded him there*	1986-90	140	51	40	.560	9	459	3.12

FIELDING

PO = Putouts

A = Assists

E = Errors

DP = Double plays

TC/G = Total chances divided by games played

FA = Fielding average

Left-Handed Pitcher	PO	A	E	DP	TC/G	FA
Jerry Koosman	62	376	25	21	1.2	.946
Al Leiter	30	176	9	15	1.0	.958
Jon Matlack	35	205	7	7	1.2	.972
Sid Fernandez	22	143	5	5	0.7	.971
Bobby Ojeda	51	146	6	14	1.5	.970

ELEVEN

Relief Pitcher

On December 6, 1989, the Mets traded relief pitchers with the Cincinnati Reds in a deal that would amount to a homecoming for **John Franco**.

Born in Brooklyn, Franco attended Lafayette High School, the same school that produced Sandy Koufax and Mets owner Fred Wilpon, as well as St. John's University. He had been taken in the fifth round of the 1981 draft by the Los Angeles Dodgers and spent three seasons as a starting pitcher in their farm system until he was traded to Cincinnati in early 1983.

Franco spent six seasons in Cincinnati but never gave up his Brooklyn home or his Brooklyn roots, and then, in 1990, he was coming home as an established star relief pitcher to save games for the New York Mets, right in his backyard.

Ostensibly, the trade was Franco for Randy Myers, which appeared to be a standoff. There was little to differentiate between them. Both were left-handed relief specialists who had thrived in the role of closer. The previous year, Myers had won seven games and saved 24 for the Mets, while Franco had won four games and saved 32 for the Reds. At 28, Franco was two years older than Myers and a little more experienced.

1. JOHN FRANCO

2. TUG McGRAW

3. JESSE OROSCO

4. BILLY WAGNER

5. ROGER McDOWELL

John Franco was lights out. He saved 276 games for the Mets over 14 seasons.

In six seasons in Cincinnati, he had won 42 games and saved 148. In four seasons with the Mets, the rapidly improving Myers had 17 wins and 56 saves.

The biggest difference between the two left-handers was their paychecks. Franco, who had reached arbitration-eligible status, was earning seven figures annually. Myers was barely over the major league minimum, about one-third of Franco's take.

Franco and Myers would both go on to have outstanding careers. Myers would record 347 saves in 14 seasons with six different teams. He would save 53 games for the Cubs in 1993 and 45 for the Orioles in 1997, both times winning Fireman of the Year honors.

Franco never saved more than 39 games in any season, but after the trade he would pitch for 15 more years, all but one with the Mets, for whom he saved 276 games. He would play past his 45th birthday and finish with 424 saves, fourth on the major league's all-time list behind Trevor Hoffman, Lee Smith, and Mariano Rivera, and first among left-handed relievers.

Now you might say that there were other relievers who came before Johnny and pitched two and three innings and never got the chance to pile up the save numbers like the modern-day relievers do. That's true. Franco pitched in the era when, if you're the closer, you come into a game in the ninth inning with a three-run lead or less and you're *the* guy. It's that sort of specialization that has produced what purists refer to as "cheap" saves.

That may be true, but it's not the closer's fault he's used in that manner, and it's certainly nothing for which Franco needs to apologize. He was called on to do a job, and he did it better than most. Case closed. Simply stated, John Franco was an outstanding relief pitcher.

He had guts and the perfect temperament for a closer. When someone is so high up on the all-time list and has the most saves for a left-hander in the history of the game, that says something. You have to give Franco his due; he did it, and he was a big part of what the Mets accomplished for a long time.

This has nothing to do with Franco's place as a relief pitcher, but I want to make mention of it. I'm involved with a foundation that helps widows and children of New York City policemen and firemen killed in the line of duty. Each year we hold a picnic fund-raiser at which we try to get as many Mets to attend as possible. When Johnny was with the Mets, he was my go-to guy in getting players to attend the picnic. As a veteran player and a native New Yorker, he took it upon himself to get players to attend and help make the affair a success. I just want him to know how much I appreciate that.

Two things come immediately to mind when I think about **Tug McGraw**: slapping his glove against his leg as he walked off the field after winning or saving a game that was both an act of celebration and a signal of greeting to his wife in the stands, and his emotion, yelling and screaming and exhilarating in all kinds of situations.

The Tugger. I loved him. He was a man of extreme highs and extreme lows, and I was very pleased to call him a friend. You should have seen him reciting "Casey at the Bat," dressed in a tuxedo, accompanied by a symphony orchestra. It was Tug at his best.

The Tugger. I loved him. You should have seen him reciting "Casey at the Bat," dressed in a tuxedo, accompanied by a symphony orchestra. It was Tug at his best.

There are relief pitchers with better records and more saves for the Mets, but none was as big a part of the Mets' legacy as kooky, wacky, flaky, lovable Tug McGraw.

In nine seasons, Tug saved 86 games for the Mets. There are several reasons why he didn't save more than that.

1. He came up in 1965 primarily as a starting pitcher and started 21 games for the Mets in his first two seasons, 36 in his nine seasons with them.
2. Initially, once he became a relief pitcher exclusively, McGraw, a left-hander, split the closer's role with Ron Taylor, a right-hander.
3. Tug pitched on a Mets team that had Tom Seaver, Jerry Koosman, Nolan Ryan, Gary Gentry, and Jon Matlack—pitchers who believed in finishing what they started and preferred to close out their own games rather than turn them over to a reliever.
4. He pitched in an era when managers let starting pitchers finish what they started and closers were not used as they are in today's game, when they are put in a game in the ninth inning with a three-run lead and nobody on base.

Case in point: check out Tug's record in 1973, when he was the Mets' exclusive closer. In the regular season, he finished second in the National League in saves with 25 (the Mets had 47 complete games) and pitched 118⅔ innings in 60 games, or two innings per outing.

Then in the postseason that year he pitched 4⅓ innings in Game 4 of the National League Championship Series against the Reds. The next day, he came back to retire two batters with the bases loaded and save Tom Seaver's victory in the pennant-clincher. After two days off, Tug pitched two innings in Game 1 of the World Series against Oakland. The next day, he entered the game in the sixth inning and pitched six innings and was the winning pitcher in the Mets' 10–7, twelfth-inning victory. Four days later, he worked 2⅔ innings in Game 5, and two days after that, finished up with one inning in Game 6.

As much as he did on the mound for the Mets during the regular season and the postseason of 1973, it was something he said in the clubhouse during that season for which Tug will always be remembered.

He was a heck of a pitcher, but it was Tug McGraw's vibrant personality that left the most indelible mark on the team. *Photo courtesy of Getty Images.*

It was August and we were struggling to win games, at the bottom of the National League East division. M. Donald Grant, the Mets' chairman of the board, decided he should address the team and give us a pep talk. These kinds of things rarely do a team any good, but this one did—only not through any wisdom or motivation imparted by Grant.

Grant kept telling us that despite our record and our position in the standings, he had confidence in us. He said he believed in us and that the owner of the team, Joan Payson, believed in us. And he told us we had to believe in ourselves. He kept using that phrase over and over, that we have to believe.

When Grant left the room, Tug stood up in front of his locker and kept shouting, "You gotta believe! You gotta believe!"

When he did that, everybody in the room had to bail into their lockers because we were all hysterical. I had to turn my face around; I was laughing so hard I couldn't breathe. I had my face in my locker and a towel around my face trying hard not to let anybody see or hear me laughing hysterically.

What McGraw didn't realize was that Grant was just outside the locker room door, and when he heard Tug shouting, "You gotta believe," he came back into the room. Buddy Harrelson had gone to Tug and told him, "You better apologize to Mr. Grant, because he thinks you were making fun of him."

Was Tug mocking Grant? That depends on whom you talk to. Let's just say it was simply Tug being exuberant. When Grant confronted him, McGraw denied he was poking fun at him. He convinced Grant that he was just echoing the chairman's suggestion that the players believe in themselves and added that just a few weeks before, a Catholic nun had preached the same motto of belief in oneself.

Tug got away with it. The explanation seemed to satisfy Grant, and the phrase, "You gotta believe," entered the Mets' lexicon and became a rallying cry for the rest of the season as we surged from last place to finish first in the division and then made it to the World Series. Tug, bless him, had turned what could have been a negative situation into a positive one and, at the same time, became a legendary figure in Mets folklore.

When Jerry Koosman had attained veteran status and demanded a trade to the Twins in his native Minnesota, it left the Mets with little leverage. The deal was made after the 1978 season with Koosman going to Minnesota and the Mets getting a minor league player and a player to be named later.

The "player to be named later" turned out to be a skinny, 21-year-old left-handed pitcher with only one season of professional ball in a rookie league under his belt and whose inclusion in the deal caused hardly a ripple in the baseball waters. Who could have known back then that the young left-hander named **Jesse Orosco** would go on to pitch for 24 years in the major leagues with nine different teams and would retire at the ripe, old, pipe-and-slippers age of 46 after appearing in more games than any other pitcher in major league history, 1,252?

Jesse's longevity shows that if you're a good person, you're loose with your team, you're a veteran, you stay in shape, and you're a left-hander who can get left-handed hitters out, you're always going to be able to get a job. Teams are constantly searching for specialty left-handed pitchers who can get out

Jesse Orosco has pitched more games—1,252—than any major league pitcher, but Mets fans remember him best as the guy who recorded the final out in Game 7 of the 1986 World Series. *Photo courtesy of Getty Images.*

left-handed hitters, and Orosco built himself quite a résumé. He had been there, done that, and proved that he could do it in clutch situations.

The first eight of Orosco's 24 major league seasons were spent with the Mets, where he shared the closer's role, first with Doug Sisk and later with Roger McDowell. As a result of that split, Orosco recorded only 107 saves, but still he was the Mets' all-time saves leader at the time of his trade to the Dodgers after the 1987 season.

Jesse's best season as a Met was 1984 when he saved 31 games, third best in the National League, but his legacy as a Mets hero was forged in the 1986 postseason. During the regular season, manager Davey Johnson did a good job of juggling his two relievers and making certain they each got enough work to stay sharp. McDowell pitched in 75 games, won 14, and saved 22; Orosco pitched in 58 games, won eight, and saved 21.

When the National League Championship Series and the World Series came around, Davey, like all good managers, played the hot hand. And Orosco was the one who had it at the time. In the best-of-seven NLCS against Houston he pitched seven innings and won three games over a span of five days. In the World Series, Jesse pitched in four of the seven games and saved two of them.

Can you imagine that? Orosco was on the mound in Houston on October 15 when the Mets clinched the National League pennant, and he was on the mound in Shea Stadium 12 days later when the Mets clinched their second World Series championship. What a thrill that had to be for Jesse. What Mets fan will ever tire of seeing the film of Jesse striking out Marty Barrett for the final out of the seventh game of the World Series and then flinging his glove into the air—I didn't think you could throw a glove that high—and then dropping to his knees on the mound, his arms thrust heavenward in triumphant celebration?

Billy Wagner's major league career has come full circle. He made his major league debut against the Mets as a Houston Astro in 1995, and 11 years later he became a Met when he signed with them as a free agent.

Wagner's 2008 season was cut short when he tore a ligament in his left elbow. He left with 385 saves, 39 short of Franco's record for the most saves by a left-hander. Wagner will miss the entire 2009 season after undergoing Tommy John surgery, leaving his career and his chance of breaking Franco's record in doubt.

If Billy Wagner can stay healthy, he has a good chance of eclipsing John Franco's record for the most saves by a left-handed pitcher.

All closers have some painful games—it's the nature of the beast—but Billy has consistently been one of the top save pitchers in baseball. He's a guy with a great arm and awesome stuff that has occasionally registered 100 miles an hour on the radar gun.

Granted, Wagner has the advantage of pitching in the era of specialization in which a closer rarely enters a game before the ninth inning and most often with nobody on base and a three-run lead. Still, he is a six-time All-Star; has had eight seasons with 30 saves or more; is fourth on the Mets' all-time saves list behind Franco, Armando Benitez, and Orosco; and is third behind Benitez's 43 and 41 saves for the most saves in a season, with 40 in 2006.

When his career is over, there's a good chance that Wagner will be among the top four saves leaders in baseball history, and he may even eclipse Franco's record of 424 for the most saves by a left-hander.

As he watched Billy Wagner pile up the saves, threatening his record of 424 for the most saves ever by a left-hander, John Franco was conflicted.

"I know records are made to be broken," he said, "and I expect Billy to pass me some day. I'm not rooting against him, but I'm hoping he doesn't do it before the year 2010."

Why 2010? Because that's the year Franco becomes eligible for the Baseball Hall of Fame, and he realizes his chances of reaching Cooperstown are better if he is the all-time saves leader among left-handed pitchers.

"I have great respect for Billy Wagner," Franco said. "What I like about him is that he challenges hitters. And for a small guy, as powerful as he is for his size, he throws in the upper nineties. That always impressed me about him. From the time he came up, he threw very hard, and he's always been among the best relief pitchers. Challenging hitters, his ability to throw hard, and that nasty slider is what has made him such a good relief pitcher year in and year out.

"I don't see much similarity between me and Billy, except that we're both left-handed. Billy is a power guy, and I was more of a finesse guy. When I first came up, I threw in the low nineties, but consistently I was between 88 and 90. Wagner came up throwing 95, 96 miles an hour. The difference between us is that I would try to trick hitters, and he challenges them—he tries to throw the ball by them.

"I'm glad I was the type of pitcher I was," Franco said. "If I had thrown that hard, I might have gotten caught up in the numbers and I might have tried to throw harder and harder. I think of myself as more of a pitcher than a thrower, and I always thought of those guys that hit 98 miles an hour on the gun as throwers.

"I tend to believe that guys that throw hard don't last as long. Billy has been a rare case, throwing hard and being a dominant reliever for so many years. But now he's hurt (out with a torn ligament in his left elbow, facing surgery, his career, and his chances of breaking Franco's record, in jeopardy). It makes you wonder if all those years of throwing so hard has started to take its toll.

"I'm proud of the fact that I had a long career (21 years), and that might not have been the case if I threw hard.

"When I look at other relief pitchers, the one I feel was more like me is Jesse Orosco. He wasn't a hard thrower, but he had a great slider and curveball, and he spotted his fastball. And look at how long Jesse lasted (24 years)."

Roger McDowell was the kind of flaky, blithe spirit that we have come to learn is common among relief pitchers. He was a prankster in the mold of other relievers such as Tug McGraw, Al Hrabosky, and Sparky Lyle.

When the Mets' offense fizzled, Roger was known to set off firecrackers in the bat rack to "wake up" the bats. Once, during a nationally televised game, he appeared wearing his uniform upside down, his pants over his head and his shoes on his upstretched hands. It was that sort of kookiness that helped him keep his cool in the pressure situations that closers often face.

McDowell was drafted by the Mets in the third round of the June 1982 draft and reached Shea Stadium three years later, sharing closer's duty with Jesse Orosco. Over the next three seasons, McDowell and Orosco won a combined 46 games and saved 118 for the Mets.

Can you see a manager doing that today? By the nature of his job, a closer has to have an ego, and his ego would never permit him to share the spotlight. Roger and Jesse liked each other and they were able to work together, but they both had an ego, they both wanted the job, and they both battled for it.

The closer's job is too difficult to expect to get it done by committee. Having two pitchers share the closer's role would never work today, and it wouldn't have worked a quarter of a century ago either if it weren't for the way Davey Johnson handled it.

It wasn't easy. McDowell and Orosco both were both so good that they both deserved the job. So Johnson had to walk a fine line. He had to figure out how to use them, when to use Jesse and when to use Roger. He had to massage their egos. He had to make sure they both got enough work to stay sharp. And he had to give each of them their chance to be in the spotlight. He had to analyze what hitters were coming up for the opposition, who the other team had on the bench, what matchups were best…all those things. He

Roger McDowell's antics kept the guys in stitches. He and fellow closer Jesse Orosco proved to be a winning combination for a championship season.

had to make sure he didn't shoot his guns too early and be left without either of them at the end. And Davey handled it all very skillfully.

There were many times when McDowell and Orosco both pitched in the same game, and one time in particular that was memorable.

It was in Cincinnati, midway through the 1986 season. The Mets and Reds hooked up in a close game that was tied at 3–3 after nine innings, when suddenly manager Davey Johnson found himself running out of players. He had used four pitchers. He had also lost Darryl Strawberry in the sixth inning when Straw was ejected for arguing a called third strike. Then he lost Ray Knight and Kevin Mitchell, who were tossed out after being involved in a brawl.

In the bottom of the tenth inning, in came Orosco, the fifth Mets pitcher of the game. The Reds got a runner to third base with two outs, and the next batter was rookie Wade Rowdon, a right-handed hitter. The obvious move was to bring McDowell in to face the right-handed hitting Rowdon, but Johnson knew that if he did that, he would lose Orosco and he would be left without a left-handed pitcher to face the left-handed hitters.

So Davey decided to improvise. He brought in McDowell to face Rowdon, but instead of removing Orosco from the game, Davey sent him to right field. This went on for four more innings. When there was a right-handed hitter coming to bat, McDowell would come in to pitch and Orosco would go to the outfield. When a left-handed hitter was batting for the Reds, Orosco would come in to pitch and McDowell would go to the outfield (right field if the hitter was right-handed, left field if the hitter was left-handed).

The Mets finally won it, 6–3, with three runs in the fourteenth. When the game ended, Gary Carter, who had started at catcher, was playing third base; Mookie Wilson, who started in left field, switched to right field, and was shuttled between left and right field with every pitching change, was back in left; Orosco was playing right field; and McDowell was pitching.

In the 1986 championship season, Roger appeared in more games than Orosco (75 vs. 58), won more (14 vs. 8), and saved more (22 vs. 21), but in the spirit of détente, Orosco outdid McDowell in the postseason with his three wins in the National League Championship Series and two saves in the World Series.

McDowell, however, was not without his moments of glory. He pitched two hitless innings in Game 4 of the NLCS against Houston and five one-hit innings in the famous and pivotal sixteen-inning Game 6 victory that clinched the pennant.

In the World Series against the Red Sox, Roger pitched two shutout innings in Game 1, two hitless innings in Game 3, and when Orosco struck out Marty Barrett for the final out in the seventh game, the win Orosco saved belonged to his counterpart as Mets closer, Roger McDowell.

Statistical Summaries

All statistics are from player's Mets career only.

PITCHING

G = Games
W = Games won
L = Games lost
PCT = Winning percentage
SV = Saves
SO = Strikeouts
ERA = Earned run average

Relief Pitcher	Years	G	W	L	PCT	SV	SO	ERA
John Franco *Only Met to lead league in saves (1990-2001, 2003-2004)*	1990-2004	695	48	56	.462	276	592	3.10
Tug McGraw *Had a 2.24 ERA in 26 postseason appearances*	1965-67, 69-74	361	47	55	.461	86	618	3.17
Jesse Orosco *Finished 3rd in 1983 Cy Young Award voting*	1979, 81-87	372	47	47	.500	107	506	2.73

continued	Years	G	W	L	PCT	SV	SO	ERA
Billy Wagner *Allowed just 555 hits in 818 career innings*	2006-08	181	5	5	.500	101	226	2.40
Roger McDowell *Winning pitcher in Game 7 of 1986 World Series*	1985-89	280	33	29	.532	84	228	3.13

FIELDING

PO = Putouts

A = Assists

E = Errors

DP = Double plays

TC/G = Total chances divided by games played

FA = Fielding average

Relief Pitcher	PO	A	E	DP	TC/G	FA
John Franco	34	132	4	8	0.2	.976
Tug McGraw	42	120	15	7	0.5	.915
Jesse Orosco	25	82	2	6	0.3	.982
Billy Wagner	3	20	1	0	0.2	.958
Roger McDowell	65	105	6	7	0.6	.965

TWELVE

Manager

Gil Hodges came out of Princeton, Indiana, and signed with the Brooklyn Dodgers as a third baseman in 1943, at the age of 19. He came up at the end of the '43 season to play one game at third base for the Dodgers and then, like many major league players in his day, left for the war, where he spent three years with the Marines as a platoon leader in the South Pacific.

When he returned in 1947, the Dodgers had made Hodges a catcher, but the arrival of Roy Campanella caused the Dodgers to convert Hodges again, this time to a first baseman.

Explained Dodgers manager Leo Durocher, "With my catching set, I put a first baseman's glove on our other rookie catcher, Gil Hodges, and told him to have some fun. Three days later, I looked up and, wow, I was looking at the best first baseman I'd seen since Dolph Camilli."

Hodges became a mainstay on those great Dodgers teams of the 1950s, the strong, silent type, a modern-day Lou Gehrig. He was an eight-time All-Star and a three-time Gold Glove winner (he would have won more, but the Gold

1.	GIL HODGES
2-T.	BOBBY VALENTINE
2-T.	DAVEY JOHNSON
4.	CASEY STENGEL
5.	WILLIE RANDOLPH

Gil Hodges (second from left) was a respected leader whose time was far too short. He's shown here in 1967 with (from left) Mets president Bing Devine, coach Yogi Berra, and coach Joe Pignatano.

Glove wasn't created until 1957, Gil's 10th major league season). He drove in more than 100 runs in seven consecutive seasons, hit more than 20 home runs for 11 consecutive seasons, hit four home runs in a game against the Milwaukee Braves on August 31, 1950, and held the National League record for grand-slam home runs with 14 when he retired.

With a lifetime batting average of .273, 370 career home runs, and 1,274 RBIs, many call Hodges "the greatest player not in the Hall of Fame."

Hodges was such a beloved figure that when he was hitless for 21 at-bats in the 1952 World Series, he elicited sympathy rather than scorn. His slump continued into the following season, and legend has it that on one steamy Sunday morning, a priest celebrating mass in a Catholic church in Brooklyn announced from the pulpit, "It's too hot for a sermon, so just say a prayer for Gil Hodges."

To further endear him to Dodgers fans, Hodges met and married a Brooklyn girl, Joan Lombardi, and made Brooklyn his permanent home even after he and the Dodgers moved to Los Angeles.

In keeping with their plan to stock their team with familiar names and former New York heroes, the Mets selected Hodges as a charter member of the team in the 1961 expansion draft. Hodges would hit the first home run in Mets history, on April 11, 1962, in St. Louis, but age (he was 38) and injury had taken their toll. He would play in only 54 games that season and hit only eight more home runs. In 1963, he played in only 11 games when he was traded to the Washington Senators, who wanted Hodges to be their manager.

In Washington, Hodges took over an expansion team in its third year and finished 10th. But he improved the team in each of the next four seasons and, in 1967, his Senators won 76 games and finished sixth in the American League. Meanwhile, the Mets continued to flounder under Casey Stengel and Wes Westrum and had designs on bringing Hodges back as their manager. But the Senators, happy with what Hodges had accomplished, had signed him to a long-term contract and were reluctant to let him go despite Hodges' desire to return home to New York.

Eventually, the Senators relented and let Hodges go to the Mets in exchange for $150,000 and pitcher Bill Denehy. Hodges became the manager of the Mets in 1968, taking over a team that had never finished higher than ninth and never won more than 66 games in their six years in the National League.

In his first season as their manager, Hodges improved the Mets by 12 games, but they still finished ninth. The following season, he pulled off one of the greatest upsets in baseball history. I was with the Expos in 1969, and I watched with amazement as Hodges led the Mets to 100 wins and a pennant, leading National League East by eight games. He then led them to a sweep of the Braves in the National League Championship Series, and then, after losing the first game of the World Series, they came back to win four straight from the heavily favored Baltimore Orioles for the Mets' first World Series championship.

They were the "Miracle Mets" of 1969, and Hodges was hailed as a miracle worker. An imposing figure at 6'2", 210 pounds, Hodges was a man of quiet strength who ruled by intimidation. You did things his way, or you didn't play for him.

Although the Mets slipped to third place with identical 83–79 records in each of the next two years, Hodges remained the strongman of the Mets, he continued to earn the respect, admiration, affection, and loyalty of all those who played for him.

At his untimely death on Easter Sunday, 1972, Hodges was at the peak of his power and in the prime years for a manager. Had he lived, there's no telling how long he would have continued as manager of the Mets or how many more World Series he might have won.

Here I go again. I'm torn between **Bobby Valentine** and **Davey Johnson** for the number two spot as Mets manager behind Gil Hodges. So, kindly bear with me as I hedge and pick Johnson and Valentine in a tie for second.

Both were outstanding and successful managers, but the curious thing is that they did it with different styles. It would be hard to find two managers who were almost equally successful and yet earned their success with completely different approaches.

Davey won more games as manager of the Mets than anybody else, 595, and he had the highest winning percentage of any Mets manager, .588. He

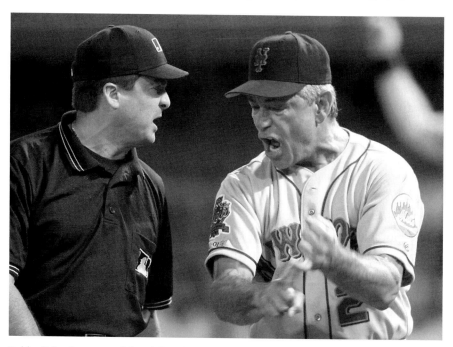

Bobby Valentine was quick to bring the fire as a manager. He would be ejected from plenty of games during his tenure—but only once did he return to the dugout in disguise.

Davey Johnson's low-key style of managing proved effective for the Mets teams of the mid-1980s.

won a World Series and two division titles, but I always felt his teams under-performed. They should have won more championships than they did. They were that good.

Bobby is second to Johnson for most wins as manager of the Mets with 536 and third behind Johnson and Willie Randolph for the highest winning percentage as manager of the Mets at .534. He never won a division title, but he did win a pennant and he got the Mets to the World Series against the Yankees in 2000.

Valentine came out of Stamford, Connecticut, where he was a celebrated three-sport star, so good that the Dodgers took him in the first round, the number five pick in the country, in the 1968 draft. He had hundreds of scholarship offers from the biggest football factories in the country, but he turned them all down to play baseball.

He was on his way to becoming a major star when he tore up his leg going all-out to catch a ball and smashed into a wall while playing for the Angels. His leg was so mangled that he was never the same after that. He bounced around to three other teams including the Mets before finally hanging it up and concentrated on becoming a manager. Being in the dugout as a manager was his answer to the disappointment of not living up to his potential as a player because of his injury. He wanted badly to be a manager, and he worked at it.

When his playing career ended, Valentine served as a minor league instructor, first with the Padres and then with the Mets, who brought him to New York as their third-base coach under George Bamberger, Frank Howard, and Davey Johnson, until the Texas Rangers made him their manager early in the 1985 season.

He took over a team that had finished seventh in the American League West the previous year and would finish seventh again. But by the next year, he had the Rangers in contention, finishing second, five games out of first. Bobby spent parts of eight seasons in Texas and managed and won more games than any manager in Rangers history.

When he left Texas, Bobby returned to the Mets in 1994 as manager of their top farm team in Norfolk. After a year, he left to manage Chiba Lotte in the Japanese League for a year and then returned to manage Norfolk again in 1996. On August 26 of that year, Valentine became the Mets 16th manager, replacing Dallas Green.

As a manager, Bobby was fiery. He grew up in the Dodgers organization, and as a young player he got the benefit of all that great Dodger training. In those days, the Dodgers set the standard in baseball for fundamentals, and everybody was trying to copy the Dodgers' methodical ways in which every player in their organization did everything one way: the Dodger way. Bobby was a student and a disciple of those Dodgers principles. He was very bright, and he became something of an innovator.

He brought the Mets to a championship level at a time when a lot of people doubted the Mets could reach such heights. In 1997, his first full year as the Mets' manager, he improved them by 17 games. Three years later, he had the Mets in the World Series against the Yankees, and I don't think anybody predicted that.

Bobby challenged everybody. He challenged his players, he challenged the other team, he challenged the media. He likes showing people that he is smart—and he is smart. I truly respect Bobby's knowledge of the game, and I like him for more than his baseball knowledge. Unbeknownst to most people, he is one of the most giving guys I've ever been around as far as helping people with different problems in their lives and in supporting many charities. Bobby is incredibly giving, and I grew to care a great deal about him.

With Valentine, there is no middle ground, especially when it comes to his relationship with the media. They either like him or they can't stand him, nothing in between.

There are some members of the media that I really like who dislike Bobby, and they would say to me, "How can you like that guy?" And I would say, "You don't like him because you don't know him the way I know him. He's one of the greatest guys in the world. You know him as the manager of the ballclub, and you're adversarial to start with." That's the way it is; the media is an adversary of every manager in baseball. I know Valentine for all his great works and the fact is that he has a terrific baseball mind—not good, terrific.

Bobby challenged everybody. He challenged his players, he challenged the other team, he challenged the media.

By the same token, there are members of the media who are very fond of Bobby and are very loyal to him. That's Bobby. If you know him, he engenders that loyalty. The Bobby Valentine I know can be very charming and very personable and, as I said, one of the greatest people I know.

That is not to be taken as a knock on Davey Johnson. Don't get me wrong, I love Davey, too—as a manager and as a man. I have respect for both Johnson and Valentine for what they were able to do with their teams. They're just different, that's all.

Davey did it by being relaxed and not having a whole lot of rules. I just thought that his lack of discipline was evident in the lack of discipline on his club. He had a great team in 1986. They killed everybody that year, and with that team, they should have won more championships.

Maybe the Mets needed a little more discipline during that era. Maybe if they'd have had that discipline, they wouldn't have had the problems they had off the field. They were a team that should have dominated for five or six years, but instead they made the playoffs only twice.

They used to talk about the "McReynolds Patch" and the "Strawberry Patch," where those two players would stand in one spot on every hitter and never move. Davey's response to that was, "You can't make someone go away from what they feel comfortable with." That was his way of coming to the defense of his players. Valentine wouldn't have sat by without doing something about it. He would have had somebody talking to McReynolds and Strawberry to convince them that they had to move around, they had to adjust to the hitter and to the pitcher, not just stand in one spot and wear down the grass.

Yet both managers had success in their own right. Davey won a World Series with the Mets, he finished first twice, he won a division title and was Manager of the Year in Baltimore, and he won with the Dodgers. Guys liked playing for him. Was his style right and Valentine's style wrong? Was Valentine's style right and Johnson's style wrong? Who knows? What their success with such different styles tells me is that there's more than one way to manage and win.

Johnson had an excellent playing career for 13 seasons as a second baseman for the Orioles, Braves, Phillies, and Cubs. He won three Gold Gloves; made the All-Star team four times; and in 1973, playing in Atlanta's home-run palace, he set the major league record for home runs by a second baseman with 42. Two years later, he went to Japan to play for the Yomiuri Giants and became the only guy to play with both Sadahuru Oh and Henry Aaron, at the time the two most prolific home-runs hitters in baseball history.

When his playing days were over, Johnson went to work for the Mets as a minor league manager. Frank Cashen, who knew Davey when they were together in Baltimore, brought Davey to the Mets, and he managed their Jackson team in the Texas League to a pennant. Then he took the Mets' top farm team, the Tidewater Tides, to the Governor's Cup title and the Triple A World Series championship in 1983. The following year he became the Mets' 11th manager, succeeding Frank Howard.

Davey grew up in the Orioles' organization and played there under Earl Weaver, so it was natural that he adopted a lot of Weaver's philosophy when he became a manager. Like Weaver, Davey didn't do a lot of bunting or play much of the hit-and-run, but he relied on pitching, defense, and the three-run homer because that's what he was accustomed to. He was successful in his own right and left his mark on the Mets.

In his first year as manager of the Mets, he improved the team by 22 games and finished second in the National League East with a record of 90–72. He became the first manager in baseball history to win at least 90 games in each of his first five years.

Johnson earned a mathematics degree from San Antonio's Trinity University and was one of the first managers to make use of computers to compile statistical data of his team's players, as well as its opponents'.

Prior to joining their organization, Davey had one memorable connection to the Mets. Playing for the Orioles, he hit the fly ball that nestled in the glove of Mets left fielder Cleon Jones—the final out that clinched the Mets' first World Series championship in 1969. The Mets would not win another World Series until 17 years later when they beat the Boston Red Sox—with a team managed by Davey Johnson.

No doubt it will surprise some people that I have chosen among the top five managers in Mets history a man who won 175 games and lost 404, a "winning" percentage of .302 in four seasons with the Mets, and who was known to occasionally fall asleep on the bench during games. But that man is **Charles Dillon (Casey) Stengel**, the famed left-handed dentist from Kansas City, Missouri, one of the truly great characters and ambassadors of the game in the history of baseball and one of its great managerial geniuses.

The first manager of the Mets, Stengel was more than just a manager. He was a pioneer, a trailblazer, a spokesman, and a public relations tool for the team. Stengel recognized from the start that his main function was to charm and entertain the media, win over fans, and deflect attention away from his ragtag collection of over-the-hill stars, has-beens, and never-weres that he knew would comprise a horrible team. He did all that with humor, with stories of bygone days that were calculated to distract, and by obfuscation with his unique form of double-speak known as "Stengelese."

When the first-year Mets would win a game (a rarity for a team that lost its first nine games and wound up losing 120 games that season) Stengel would prance around the clubhouse praising his team and calling them "Amazin'." That's how they first became known as "The Amazin' Mets," and they are still "The Amazin' Mets" today.

Stengel was born two centuries ago, in 1890, and made his major league playing debut almost 100 years ago with the Brooklyn Dodgers. He had studied to be a dentist, but he turned to baseball and had a career that spanned 14 years as a speedy, good-fielding outfielder with the Dodgers, Pirates, Phillies, Giants, and Braves, posting a career batting average of .284.

By the time he reached the Mets, Stengel had earned his stripes with 21 years as a major league manager on both sides of the spectrum with the Boston Braves, Brooklyn Dodgers, and New York Yankees. In nine years as a manager in Boston and Brooklyn, he had one winning season and never finished higher than fifth place. With the Yankees, he became a genius,

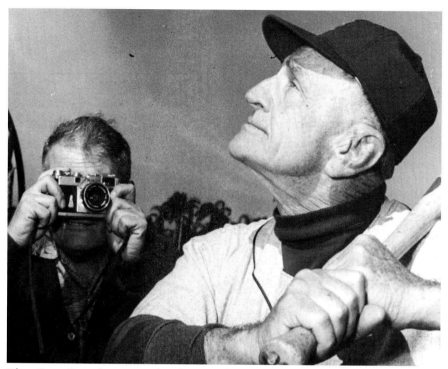

When Casey Stengel was tapped as the Mets' first manager, he needed no introduction to New York fans. He brought with him the same whimsy that he had with the Yankees, as well as the fidelity to his players and shrewd managerial insight he was known for.

188

dubbed "The Ol' Perfessor," by winning 10 American League pennants and seven World Series in 12 years.

When the Yankees lost the 1960 World Series in seven games to the Pirates, the Yankees invoked a little-known organization rule that supposedly required mandatory retirement for employees over the age of 70 (Stengel had just passed his 70th birthday). The Yankees announced his retirement, to which Casey sardonically responded, "I'll never make the mistake of turning 70 again."

A year later, while the Mets were in the process of putting together their brand-new expansion franchise, they enlisted George Weiss to run their baseball operation. Weiss had built the Yankees' dynasty of the '50s and '60s. It was Weiss who had defied baseball logic by hiring the 58-year-old Stengel, who had been managing the Oakland Oaks of the Pacific Coast League, to manage the Yankees in 1949.

I'm not including Yogi Berra in my rankings of Mets managers because Yogi is beyond category. He's in his own category, with the Mets and in baseball.

He is, in fact, "the Pope of Baseball," an elder statesman of the game, one of the most beloved and most recognized personalities in baseball history. He is unsullied by scandal and controversy, without an enemy or a detractor. Yogi is the Raymond and the Sara Lee of baseball: everybody loves Raymond, and everybody loves Yogi. Nobody doesn't like Sara Lee, and nobody doesn't like Yogi Berra.

The world loves Yogi. *I* love Yogi. And you will never get me to say a negative word about him.

Let me begin by talking about Yogi, the player, and there's so much to say on that subject. I never saw Yogi play live, but I did watch him on television when the Yankees seemed to be on "The Game of the Week" every Saturday. I have seen film clips of him, read a lot about him, talked to quite a few old-time players who played with and against him, and I have studied his statistics.

Yogi came out of St. Louis, signed for a bonus of $500, and nobody gave him a chance to even make the major leagues. Most teams passed on him because scouts said he didn't even look like a ballplayer—he stood only 5'8" and was oddly shaped, unathletic looking, and just 190 pounds.

At first, he wasn't very graceful or nimble behind the plate, and he would swing at pitches out of the strike zone, off his shoe tops, and over his head. But he worked hard, improved as a catcher, and look at what he accomplished! A notorious "bad ball" hitter but a lethal hitter in the clutch, he had a career batting average of .285, 358 home runs, and 1,430 runs batted in; he was a 15-time All-Star, 11 as the American League's starting catcher; a three-time Most Valuable Player in the AL; and he was elected to the Hall of Fame.

Perhaps Berra's greatest attribute was that he was a winner. He played on teams that won 14 pennants and 10 World Series, he hit 12 home runs, and he drove in 39 runs in 75 World Series games, the most World Series games ever by a player. And he won two more pennants as a manager.

In 1964, as a rookie manager, he brought the Yankees back from 5½ games out of first place on August 22 to win the American League pennant. When the Yankees lost the World Series to the Cardinals in seven games, Berra was fired. The following year, he joined the Mets as a player-coach. He appeared in only four games, getting two hits in nine at bats. Acknowledging that his time had passed him by, he retired as a player.

When Gil Hodges died suddenly of a heart attack just before the start of the 1972 season, the Mets made Berra their manager, and the next year he pulled off another miracle, rallying the Mets from last place, 6½ games out of first place on August 31, to win his second pennant as a manager.

A good part of the Berra legend stems from his penchant for funny sayings, curious comments, and malaprops, which have been called "Berraisms" or "Yogi-isms" and which have become part of baseball's lexicon. Most of these comments were unintentional, and many of them were made up by others and attributed to him (Yogi once told a reporter, "I didn't say all the things I said").

One of his most famous "Berraisms" came during the latter part of the 1973 season when it appeared the Mets were destined to finish near the bottom of the National League East. Berra never lost hope, even when things looked their bleakest, and one day he told reporters, "It ain't over 'til it's over."

Yogi was right. He almost always is. That phrase became the rallying cry for the 1973 Mets; it entered the lexicon and is still used to this day. It will probably be used for generations to come by politicians, television commentators, and coaches in other sports from Little League and Pop Warner League all the way up to the major leagues and the NFL, all of them quoting baseball's noted philosopher, one Mr. Yogi Berra.

Then, in 1961 and past his 71st birthday, Stengel was being asked by Weiss to once again manage his team, New York's soon-to-be new National League franchise. Stengel would thereby become the only man ever to wear the uniform of all four of New York's major league teams, as a player for the Brooklyn Dodgers and New York Giants and a manager for the Dodgers, the New York Yankees, and New York Mets.

I regret that I never got to know Stengel, but I do remember having a few brief encounters with him, although I could never figure out what he was saying. He was always talking about money, and I was a bonus baby for the expansion Houston Colt .45s, later the Astros, which apparently caught the attention of Stengel, who was a part-owner of a bank in his hometown of Glendale, California.

I'd be jogging by him and he would say something I couldn't understand except that it had something to do with money. So, I'd say to him, "Maybe if I had my money in your bank it would be doing better."

Willie Randolph's first try as a manager ended in disaster and disappointment. It ended, as most managerial tenures usually do, when he was fired midway through the 2008 season, Willie's fourth season as the Mets' 18th manager.

While he was there, Randolph made his mark with the Mets, a record of 302–253 and a winning percentage of .544, a higher winning percentage than contemporaries Tony La Russa, Dusty Baker, Jim Leyland, and Lou Piniella. He won more games than any Mets manager except Davey Johnson, Bobby Valentine, and Gil Hodges and had a higher winning percentage than every Mets manager except Johnson.

When the Mets hired him in 2005, Randolph had been denied his chance for almost 10 years and after almost a dozen interviews, although he had paid his dues with 18 seasons as a first-rate major league second baseman and 11 years as a coach for the Yankees.

In his first year as manager, Randolph won 83 games, an improvement of 12 games over the previous season. In his second year, he won 97 games, the fifth most in Mets history, and led them to their first National League East title in 18 years.

Things began to unravel for Randolph in 2007. On September 12, the Mets were in first place by seven games with 17 games to play. On September 24, they were still in first place, but their lead had shrunk to two games. They would lose six of their last seven games and finish out of the playoffs, the worst collapse in baseball history.

When the Mets got off to a slow start in 2008, rumors of Randolph's demise began to surface. On June 17, with a record of 34–35 and in third place, 6½ games out of first, the Mets decided a change was needed. The ax fell on Randolph. He was replaced by his bench coach, Jerry Manuel.

Willie Randolph netted a .544 winning percentage with the Mets, second only to Davey Johnson.

192

The Mets responded under Manuel and were not eliminated from playoff contention until the final day of the season. Manuel deserves credit for resuscitating the team, but to include him among the five best managers in Mets history after such a small sampling would be premature. He's going to have to do it for a few more years, and I fervently hope he does. I played with Jerry in Detroit. He's a good guy and an excellent baseball man. I'd like nothing better than to one day include Jerry Manuel among the five best managers in Mets history.

Statistical Summaries

All statistics are for manager's Mets career only.

MANAGING

G = Games managed

W = Games won

L = Games lost

PCT = Winning percentage

P = Pennants

WS = World Series victories

Manager	Years	G	W	L	PCT	P	WS
Gil Hodges *His teams improved their victory total over the previous season every year from 1964 to 1969*	1968-71	649	339	309	.523	1	1
Bobby Valentine *Only Met manager to lose an All-Star Game (2001)*	1996-2002	1,003	536	467	.534	1	0

continued	Years	G	W	L	PCT	P	WS
Davey Johnson *Posted winning records for all four teams he managed—Mets, Reds, Orioles, and Dodgers*	1984-90	1,012	595	417	.588	1	1
Casey Stengel *Managed Warren Spahn in the Hall of Fame pitcher's first (1942) and final (1965) seasons*	1962-65	582	175	404	.302	0	0
Willie Randolph *His 2006 Mets led the league in stolen bases with 146*	2005-08	555	302	253	.544	0	0

Index

Entries in italics denote references to photo captions.

MIKE PIAZZA • GARY CARTER • JERRY GROTE • TO
KRANEPOOL • DAVE KINGMAN • JOHN OLERUD •
JEFFERIES • FELIX MILLAN • WALLY BACKMAN •
ORDONEZ • KEVIN ELSTER • RAFAEL SANTANA • DA
• HUBIE BROOKS • WAYNE GARRETT • CLEON JONES
• BERNARD GILKEY • CARLOS BELTRAN • MOOKIE W
• DARRYL STRAWBERRY • BOBBY BONILLA • RON
SEAVER • DWIGHT GOODEN • RON DARLING • DAV
• JON MATLACK • SID FERNANDEZ • BOBBY OJEDA •
WAGNER • ROGER McDOWELL • GIL HODGES • B
• WILLIE RANDOLPH • MIKE PIAZZA • GARY CART
• KEITH HERNANDEZ • ED KRANEPOOL • DAVE
DELGADO • JEFF KENT • GREGG JEFFERIES • FE
HARRELSON • JOSE REYES • REY ORDONEZ • KEVIN
JOHNSON • EDGARDO ALFONZO • HUBIE BROOKS •
• CLIFF FLOYD • GEORGE FOSTER • BERNARD GILKE
• TOMMIE AGEE • LENNY DYKSTRA • DARRYL STI
SHAMSKY • JOEL YOUNGBLOOD • TOM SEAVER • DW
JONES • JERRY KOOSMAN • AL LEITER • JON MATLA